FROM SURVIVING TO THRIVING
UNLOCKED

10 ACCLAIMED EXPERTS SHARE
THEIR ADVICE FOR ADAPTING
TO LIFE AFTER A CRISIS

CURATED BY SADIE RESTORICK

Unlocked: From Surviving to Thriving

Copyright ©2020

All rights reserved. No part of this publication may be reproduced, stored in a retrieval system or transmitted in any form or by any means – electronic, mechanical, photocopy, recording or any other-except for brief quotations in printed reviews, without the prior written permission of the individual author and copyright holder.

The advice and information made available in this book is not intended to replace the services of a medical professional. The information in this book is merely the respective author's expression of opinion based on personal knowledge and experience. It cannot and should not be used to diagnose or treat any medical or health condition or ailment. The authors make no representation or guarantees with respect to any information offered or provided in this book with regards to its effectiveness.

ISBN: 978-1-83853-418-9 (ebook)
ISBN: 978-1-83853-419-6 (print)

Cover Design by Hannah Whale | Hannah.whale@hotmail.co.uk
Book Interior and E-book Design by Amit Dey | amitdey2528@gmail.com

Contents

1. Foreword v
2. Foreword 2 vii
3. Helen Lawson – Resilience and Positivity in Uncertain Times 1
4. Tracey Allport – Finding Balance in an Unbalanced World 21
5. Caroline Sherlock - Diet and Lifestyle Changes for Enhancing Energy, Balancing moods, Restful Sleep and A Robust Immune System 40
6. Sadie Restorick – The Power of Human Connection and Open Communication 65
7. Lucy Batham-Read – Trauma and Us 81
8. Marilyn Devonish – Remote Working 95
9. Steve Hoblyn – Self Awareness During Difficult Times 109
10. Imogen Tinkler – Growing Happiness 144
11. Tracey Allport – Sleeping Soundly 158
12. Sacha Mulligan – Maintaining a Positive State of Mind 172
13. Paul Dorrington - Lessons from Evidence Based Supported Employment - A Surviving and Thriving at Work Toolkit 180

Foreword

What will you remember the most when you look back on the year 2020?

For every person reading this, that answer may be different. We have, after all, all had quite different experiences and faced very unique and exceptional challenges. As such, our perception of the pandemic and way that we perceive the events that unfolded may vary greatly.

For me personally, I think I will remember a sense of connection and community, the overwhelming pride for the way that collectively we have come together as one against a common enemy. Despite being physically apart and unable to be close to the ones we love, we have come together and united in spirit. This great adversity has charged us with the responsibility of being more kind, more compassionate and more grateful and we have risen to the occasion. Whilst many have been greatly tested and experienced significant trauma and turmoil, for me that collective sense of humanity shines through the dark.

This overwhelming sense of community, and an innate desire to want to try and help people psychologically adjust to the changing times, was the driving force behind this book. I felt that the most powerful way to make a positive difference was to bring together a collection of experts from diverse backgrounds to contribute their absolute best advice in how people can cope both now and into the future. It was only by combining forces as a collaborative that I felt it would be possible to reflect the different needs of the population as, after all, one size doesn't fit all!

As you will go on to discover, this book is full of suggestions, ideas and practical tools to help you thrive in the future. From resilience and positive thinking to sleep hygiene, remote working and growing your own vegetables, it is a very eclectic mix of positive advice and strategies that you can adopt as part of your own personal action plan. Every chapter is unique and different and all content is the opinion of the individual author, it does not constitute any form of psychiatric and psychological treatment or therapy. However, I am confident that after reading it you will feel empowered, inspired and more able to make positive changes for your own wellbeing.

These techniques will not only help you adjust to life after lockdown but will provide you with a wealth of different ways you can positively face any crisis in your life. Not only will it arm you with a number of proverbial strings to add to your bow of resilience but it will sharpen your arrows and your focus to help you reach your target of health and happiness during the good times and the bad.

By Sadie Restorick

Foreword 2

Managing our mental health in the modern world is more important than ever. The current global crisis is a reminder that sometimes we can all face unexpected challenge and adversity and that having the tools to psychologically cope and adjust is critical. We have also been reminded during this time that compassion for others and yourself is critical to enable you to remain resilient and live a healthy and balanced life.

Within this book, there are invaluable tools and tips from a number of different perspectives to help you address this. Everyone is different and what works for one person might not necessarily work for another. We need to find what suits us and I am sure when you read the chapters you will find what you are looking for.

Self-care is imperative to your wellbeing. Once you have looked after yourself you can then help others. I do a number of different exercises to help me, and I am not talking about running a marathon or going to the gym. For me, I enjoy just walking the dogs and spending time in nature, and practising mindfulness and meditation which really relaxes the mind.

Practising gratitude every day puts things in perspective in today's world. There are many places in the world where people experience extreme financial hardship and poverty yet still appreciate life and find joy in other ways. Look around you and see what you have at your fingertips. We have abundance everywhere.

I do a daily gratitude regime and write down 10 things I am grateful for, and have affirmations dotted over my wall to help me maintain a positive mindset. If we flood our mind with positive energy and words, there is sure to be no room for negativity.

We live such busy lives and all face challenges on a regular basis but it is how you react and deal with situations that can have a huge effect on your mental state of mind. If you are in a good place yourself and feel relaxed, then you are more likely to address the issue in a calming and effective way. This would also make the people you interact with feel better, feel listened to and feel respected. You learn so much from listening to people, which helps you along your journey.

Too many times when we receive a negative response, we mirror what another person is saying and this can cause unnecessary stress, anxiety and emotional trauma.

If you are 100% genuine in your reaction or approach to others and show empathy and kindness when someone is less fortunate, having a bad day or suffering in some way, then the outcome will surely be more positive and beneficial to others. If we all had compassion we could create a ripple effect across the entire world - now wouldn't that be great? Do not forget: what you do is your choice, and no one is forcing you to make a decision.

Being comfortable in your own skin makes a huge difference to your confidence and self-esteem. Once you have achieved this you can then share with others. Self-awareness is key, as is being aligned to the universe so it responds accordingly. Stand confident in yourself and speak your truth. Think about the words and language you use when you speak to others. Ask yourself the question, "How would I feel if someone spoke to me like that – happy, or demoralised?"

I often complete random acts of kindness, just because I like making people happy. You do not know what kind of day someone is having and your kindness might just change their mood and cheer them up. I enjoy connecting with and speaking to people; it is so extremely important and you never know what you could have in common or what mutual friend you might have.

Believe in yourself that you CAN and WILL achieve anything in this world. REMOVE the word 'can't' from your vocabulary as it is only your limiting belief that is stopping you from achieving this goal and helping others feel good about themselves. If they see you happy and content, this in turn will motivate them to strive to help themselves.

Wouldn't it be great if we could create a community where everyone was kind to themselves and showed compassion to others?

I truly believe if this happened it would help with people's overall mental health and wellbeing and end the stigma, discrimination and emotional upset that we face today.

Be kind to yourself...

Be kind to others...

And sit back and watch the world become a better place.

By Liz Rotherham

Resilience and Positivity in an Uncertain World
by Helen Lawson

Resilience Unlocked

The start of 2020 will forever be recorded in history. Our lives and sense of security changed almost overnight and the waves and ripples for many of us will likely last a lifetime. One word that has cropped up repeatedly as a result, is "resilience". The world has woken up to the fact that many of us were ill-prepared. Even though change is one of life's only certainties, many of us had little in our armoury to protect us psychologically from the challenges ahead. We have encountered enormous change, we are now experiencing rapid adaptation, and this will be followed by stabilisation, tinged with a significant sense of uncertainty. None of us know how often we may have to encounter that cycle before real and lasting stability is achieved. But encounter it we will, and if we have only one weapon to fight with, resilience may be the perfect choice.

Depending on where you sit between The Silent Generation and Generation Z, your first encounters with the notion of resilience may vary. Had you picked up a dictionary to search for "resilience" in the 1960s, you would have been met with a definition of something entirely bound to the world of physics. Now however, on hearing the same word, many people will view it more as a human skill, first and foremost. This usage only emerged from the behavioural sciences as recently as the 1970s and it is this definition that we are concerned with.

Dr Stephen Marmer describes resilience as "life's shock absorbers" (Marmer, 2018). Wherever you look, definitions of resilience abound, and they vary considerably. In its simplest form, human resilience is about tolerance of stress. In The EQ Edge, it is described as

"...the ability to withstand adverse events and stressful situations without developing physical or emotional symptoms, by actively and positively coping with stress" (Stein & Book, 2011). This particular definition captures some key properties of resilience:

- It is an "ability". It can therefore be learned and developed, as opposed to a personality trait which may be more fixed.
- The use of the word "withstand", highlights that it is not a passive pursuit and some endeavour may be required.
- Reference to "events and stressful situations" encapsulates the impact of external stimuli.
- Mention of "physical and emotional symptoms" alerts us to the fact that we will encounter reactions to the stimuli. These reactions are entirely unique to the individual. Think of skydiving. This same activity would generate fear in one person and exhilaration in another.
- Finally, and perhaps most significantly, we are alerted to the pursuit of "actively and positively coping". If you removed these words from the definition, it would no longer fully and accurately define resilience. Our resilience is largely determined, not by the stressors that impact us, but by our

conscious and mentally proactive response to the event. This is the key to building and maintaining resilience.

So, resilience can be developed by everyone, whatever their starting point. It requires some fortitude against the external stimuli which create a unique response in each of us. Our job then is to identify what it is that triggers the stress response and crucially how that affects us. Only then can we begin to moderate our response into something more positive. When discussing resilience, Meg Jay said that

"People do not feel understood when someone says, 'Wow, you really bounced back from that.' They don't feel seen in all of their complexity, in terms of how hard it can be,'" (Jay, 2018).

She goes on to highlight a characteristic often attributed to resilience, the ability to bounce back from adversity. While resilience is often described as a "bounce", this conjures up an image of something which happens entirely automatically. For most of us, that is simply not the case. Jay's much more accurate analysis of the situation is that "It's really a battle, not a bounce," (Jay, 2018).

The great thing about humankind is that we have evidence that we are demonstrably resilient beings. If we weren't, we wouldn't have survived. But there is a difference between being resilient enough to survive and being sufficiently resilient to thrive. Sadly, our history is chequered with great tragedies of incomprehensible magnitude. From world wars to natural disasters, such as the Indian Ocean tsunami of 2004, we have been witness to the reality that there is a natural human instinct within us to survive. Most of us will fortunately not have to endure such trauma and hardship, but we can take heart from the knowledge that we are hardwired to pull through from adversity. It would be naïve and dismissive to suggest that people coming through such life-changing adversity can do so with a "bounce" or without scarring and that is not the suggestion.

If we know that even those who live through such experiences can survive, recover, and indeed thrive again, we can rest assured that we have the raw materials available to do likewise, while dealing with the common day to day challenges which we will encounter. And we can do this with confidence if we prepare ourselves in advance. While resilience doesn't have to be arduous, it will likely require some commitment on an ongoing basis, to become well honed, in the same way that building up a bicep requires work over time. If you stop working on that muscle, you'll retain some residual strength, but you won't be in peak condition. To maintain top form, you must apply yourself with commitment and determination.

Whatever resilience is, there is an even longer list of what it's not. It is not being happy or positive all the time. That is simply not a possibility in life. You have permission to be down sometimes, to feel disappointed, dejected or deflated. That is not a personal weakness, it is life in all its high definition glory. There are no bad emotions. We must feel emotions that are less appealing, to really appreciate those that are fantastic. Resilience is having those moments that do not fit with the plan, and still finding a way to push on through.

Resilience as a Structure for Success

Resilience is a vital coping skill for a well-rounded life experience. We will all be hit by stressful situations. Some of these may be quite minor, some may be unequivocally life changing. Nobody is immune. If we do not have the skills to cope with these events, what is our alternative? The global pandemic of 2020 created a previously unimaginable change in our way of life. Everyone, everything, everywhere was affected by the same unseen danger. The ways in which we felt personally affected, were however quite different. Just as variable were the all-important ways in which we reacted to the event.

My own experience with resilience has led me to conclude that it is one of life's most underestimated coping skills. On reflection, the "R" word only entered my vocabulary in a meaningful way, whenever I didn't want to do something. When asked questions like "Why don't you apply for that promotion?", my stock response was "No, it's not for me, I'm just not resilient enough to work at that level/cope with that stress/deal with the responsibility". It was a story I told myself and others repeatedly. It became a central part of my narrative. In fact, in large part, it defined me, and it certainly directed my actions and behaviours. It was the best excuse I'd ever found for not doing all the things I was scared of.

This approach worked for me until I watched an episode of the exceptional Oprah Winfrey's, Super Soul Sunday (Rhimes, 2015). Oprah was interviewing Shonda Rhimes, (author, and TV & film writer of such hits as Grey's Anatomy and Scandal), about her book, Year of Yes. Rhimes explained how, despite her enormous success, she had been closed to many opportunities in life, for a long time. The show wasn't categorised as being about resilience and yet it was like having a mirror held up to me. I was struck by the parallels to my own behaviour. I too, was continually saying no to experiences and opportunities.

It dawned on me that I had just excused my behaviour by labelling it as a lack of resilience. It was as if having named the limitation, allowed me to put it in a box marked "absolved of personal responsibility to change the situation". This was in stark contrast to almost every other aspect of my life, where I wholeheartedly extolled the virtues of proactivity to change what didn't satisfy you. I had a dawning that I'd created a self-fulfilling prophecy which ensured that not only was I truly not demonstrating very resilient behaviours routinely, I was also annihilating any resiliency reserves I did have, through my own self-sabotaging-talk.

I changed my attitude immediately. I was missing so much by having the default response of "no". I woke up to the fact I could become as resilient as I wanted to be. Or rather, as resilient as I was prepared to work towards. Just as most of us don't get given an education, a job, a home or a car, without working for it, it was like an epiphany that you also don't get handed a silver platter with your resilience quota either. You therefore have two choices. Accept the struggle and limitations that are attached to a lack of resilience or get to work on developing it. Just as I wouldn't resign myself to not having an income or food on the table, I was no longer going to resign myself to being without a critical life skill.

Seeing is Believing

A good way to fully understand how much difference resilience can make to your life is to identify one famous person that you feel epitomises resilience. Who would you choose?

When I ask this question in my training sessions, I'm often given some fascinating answers. An especially popular answer is the late Nelson Mandela, a man synonymous with resilience. He was someone who endured enormous hardship and injustice, with dignity, poise and perhaps most remarkably, forgiveness. He then had the determination and courage to rebuild his life and have a positive impact on others in the process. His life was truly remarkable but went well beyond what most of us would ever wish to endure, in the pursuit of building resilience.

What qualities do you notice about the resilient role model you identified? Be as specific about them as you can be. What made them stand out to you as resilient? In all the examples I've ever been presented with, there are two facts that never change. Whatever other qualities that person possesses, had they a) not encountered great adversity and b) not responded in an overwhelmingly resilient fashion to overcome it, we would almost certainly never have known their name. Without both challenge and resilience, regardless of your other gifts, you risk becoming a footnote in your own story. With it, you open the door to a life full of possibility. And it is that we should embrace, in the knowledge that the obstacles laid in our path, will help us grow and prepare for the next hurdle.

A significant problem with a lack of resilience, is that if you believe it to be true of yourself, then as with most self-limiting beliefs, you will be absolutely vindicated in your belief. You're likely to limit your exposure to new situations, experiences and people. Think about the greatest things that have ever happened in your life. Most of them won't have been dramatic moments of thunderbolts and lightening. They tend to be slow burners, processes building to a crescendo, whether that be relationships, academic achievements, jobs or growing a family. Now imagine those wonderful moments had never happened because at some stage in your endeavour, you decided you lacked the resilience to take the first, or the second or the penultimate step. The real cause for celebration here is that you will undoubtedly already have experienced some hard-won achievements in your life. That means you have a foundation of resilience on which to build.

Now consider any times that you have limited your exposure to new or challenging environments. You will never know what fantastic outcomes might have resulted from those missed encounters. One thing I do know however, is that every time you limited your experiences, you also deprived the world of what you had to offer. They didn't get your value, insight, warmth, humour, knowledge, skills and maybe even the benefit of a connection that could have changed your life, or theirs. And therein lies one of the most poignant losses associated with lacking resilience (or believing you lack it). It diminishes you as a person and deprives the world of your talents. Until you decide to change it.

Pump up the Positivity

So, what are the practical things you can do to start to build your resilience reserves? A great starting point is to become more positive about your ability to meet the challenges that life presents you. Your sense of confidence about your ability may be determined by whether you are an optimist, a realist, or a pessimist.

Do you have a solution for every problem? Or a problem for every solution? Pessimists are inclined to expect the worst and can judge optimists as a little naïve, with an inability to identify all the risks. Optimists on the other hand may be inclined to expect the best outcome in every given situation, without recognising their agency or even responsibility to influence their results. Then there are the realists, those that we largely anticipate will get the balance about right. Heidi Grant, writing for the Harvard Business Review took the view that

"… to be successful, you need to understand the vital difference between believing you will succeed, and believing you will succeed easily. Put another way, it's the difference between being a realistic optimist and an unrealistic optimist." (Grant, 2011).

Is it realistic then, to be optimistic, if you're prepared to put in a little effort too? In my experience, absolutely. In a video for

Prager University, Dr. Stephen Marmer recounted how he often asks his patients to think about the undeserved bad things that have happened in their lives, and then asks them to compare them to the unearned good things they've experienced. His conclusion, having carried out the exercise with many patients, is that the unearned good, outweighs the undeserved bad, by a ratio of about 10:1 (Marmer, 2018).

It doesn't seem unreasonable to conclude that optimism is in fact, realistic. If that would not normally be your take on the world, there is no better time than now, to incorporate this sense-check on your future assessments of situations. When you start to look for evidence that this is true, you will find it. And as you do, you will create an upward spiral of positivity which will feed your confidence that even if things don't go as you plan, you will be able to overcome any resulting obstacles. This is also a great demonstration of employing a growth mindset, which is characterised by a belief that you have the ability to learn new things and change your results as a consequence.

To really harness the power of positive thought, it can be useful to understand a principle outlined in Cognitive Behavioural Therapy by Avy Joseph, which posits that

"If your belief about yourself is good, rational and healthy, your opinion of yourself, and your thoughts, decisions and attitudes, will be constructive." (Joseph, 2009)

Imagine an equilateral triangle with its three points. The top point represents your beliefs. Moving clockwise around the triangle, the next point represents your thoughts and moving clockwise again, the final point represents your behaviours. There are arrows flowing between each of the three points. Now consider the following assessment in relation to your triangle of beliefs, thoughts and behaviours.

"... a healthy belief is flexible, consistent with reality, logical and helpful to you in terms of goal and achievement.

An unhealthy belief is rigid, inconsistent with reality, illogical and unhelpful to your wellbeing and happiness." (Joseph, 2009)

Taking the 2020 global pandemic and UK lockdown as an example, lets imagine that your beliefs about the world are full of doom and gloom - pessimism. Such negative beliefs about the world may have generated thoughts that "nothing will ever be the same again" or "I'm locked in like a prisoner". These sorts of thoughts are then likely to foster feelings including sadness, insecurity, fear, and loneliness. But the triangle of beliefs, thoughts and behaviours doesn't stop there. Each element influences the next in perpetual motion. As such, those feeling of sadness are likely to reinforce of even further negatively impact your beliefs, which may result in further unhelpful behaviours and so on, in a downward spiral.

Crucially, at any point in this triangle, you can intervene and reverse the direction of travel. If you change the thought of "I'm locked in like a prisoner" to "I'm safe in my sanctuary, my home" this will almost certainly give rise to much more positive feelings of comfort, security, and stability. These in turn can positively influence your beliefs and so the positive cycle continues upwards on this occasion.

Guard your Reserves

When confronted with significant or numerous stressors, it can be exhausting. You only have finite energy resources and competing priorities can deplete us. Our ability to think rationally may be negatively impacted. This can lead to us feeling anxious and overwhelmed, so it is important that we create a focus and eliminate any "white noise", which may be causing unhelpful energy expenditure.

One highly effective way to achieve that is to ensure that our efforts are directed only towards endeavours which are supportive of our overall wellbeing, and in turn, our resilience. For example, during the progression of the 2020 pandemic, for many, there seemed to be a lot to worry about. There was the virus itself, government response to the situation, our personal circumstances, including health, finances, relationships, and the mental strain of what the future might look like. Stephen Covey, in The 7 Seven Habits of Highly Effective People, talked about us having a "Circle of Concern" – picture a circle, literally containing all the issues which concern or affect you.

"As we look at those things within our Circle of Concern, it becomes apparent that there are some things over which we have no real control and others that we can do something about. We could identify those concerns in the latter group by circumscribing them within a smaller Circle of Influence."

"Proactive people focus their efforts on the Circle of Influence. They work on the things they can do something about." (Covey, 2015)

For Covey then, your Circle of Concern is quite large and contains all the things that might affect or worry you but within that circle, you create an additional Circle of Influence. Now you can re-evaluate your circles. Within your smaller, inner, Circle of Influence, you will place all of the things you can do something about. Everything else, over which you hold no power, will remain in the larger, outer, Circle of Concern.

In very real terms, what does this mean for us as lockdown eases? Well, within your Circle of Influence are all the things you can do to protect yourself and your family such as continuing with hand hygiene and social distancing measures. These are your actionable items, things over which you can exercise at least some control or influence. Beyond that, in your Circle of Concern, you may be worried about a second peak or government decisions. But be clear that these are things that you cannot change.

There is enormous power in identifying what you can control, what you can influence and what concerns you, but which you have no sway over, whatsoever. I tend to think of my Circle of Concern, more constructively, as my Circle of Acceptance. This very minor shift helps to remind me that there is really nothing I can do to change it, so the best way to conserve my valuable personal resources, is to acquiesce to it. This is not necessarily easy, but it is liberating to be conscious that no amount of churning the concerns over, will alter them. You can apply this thinking to all areas of your life to help retain clear focus.

By freeing up this headspace, I can then apply my attention and valuable energy to the things I can be proactive about, such as my reaction to events, and my approach to things I have a realistic possibility of influencing, such as the people in my orbit and their attitudes or behaviours. At this stage, I can begin to plan firm actions to tackle the issues I've identified. By being specific about my intentions, I gain a real sense of control and purpose and use this to direct my energy effectively. This together with the elimination of pointless preoccupation with events outside my control, conserves my reserves and reduces the likelihood of unhelpful rumination on issues beyond me.

Manage your mind

Now we have explored the likelihood that life tends to give you a higher proportion of good experiences than bad, it should be possible to plough ahead with a rational head and a positive outlook. Sadly, life is rarely this simple, especially when we may have to change some immensely powerful stories we've carried in our heads for a long time. We can spotlight these stories by listening carefully to our own self-talk.

Have you ever noticed how many conversations you have in your head daily? It will certainly be far more than the number you verbalise in a two-way dialogue. Now think about how you talk to yourself in those internal conversations. Are you a best friend to yourself or are you an over-zealous critic? A good measure of your self-talk is to consider whether the conversations you have with yourself are conversations you would have with the people you love and respect the most. If you are saying things to yourself that you would never verbalise to someone else, or that you would feel untrue, unnecessary, or unkind if received from someone else, evaluate whether your self-talk is sabotaging you.

If you're perpetuating an unhelpful, destructive and self-critical internal dialogue, identify it quickly and make it stop. If you utilise words like "always" and "never" to yourself, regularly, in a negative way, they're almost certainly unjustified, sweeping generalisations. That's not to say you can't be reflective and identify improvement opportunities for your own personal development, but if it isn't done in a constructive way – just as you would with a friend – it's likely to do more harm than good.

But how do you decide whether your evaluation of yourself or any given situation, is fair? The aim is to be objective, but that can be a challenge. It may help to try not to make yourself the object of the situation. Change your perspective as if it were someone else in the spotlight, someone you respect and care about again. This can provide some valuable distance, to gain a better perspective. Consider whether, if you were the judge and jury in this case, you would be acquitting the defendant or passing down a damning sentence. Apply the objectivity to your case, that you would if someone's very existence depended on it.

While you're at it, you might apply the same principles to sense-checking your reactions to other people, if you sometimes find yourself triggered into unhelpful responses by their actions. Your view of a given situation is never the only view. Recognising that others' impacts on you may not be intentional, malicious, negligent, or indeed as severe as you initially perceived them, can ease tensions and build relationships. Particularly at a time when our experiences can be so vastly different, this perspective taking can be enormously valuable. Imagine for example the opposing perspectives that might be taken by two colleagues, one furloughed and one left at work. The furloughed may wonder why they were side-lined, the working wonder why they must take all the strain. For each position, there is a polar opposite, but equally valid and real lived experience that the other got the better deal. The ability to acknowledge these perspectives, helps build your emotional intelligence and build your resilience in turn.

It's also extremely helpful to tune in to your feelings. We have established that we experience physiological reactions to events or circumstances. These reactions may cause sensations in our body that we interpret simply as stress. We need to identify and label the specific emotion we're encountering, rather than just the reaction or stress response it provokes. Is it fear, is it frustration, or could it be anger? This process can take some time as you need to allow yourself to fully experience the feeling before you can name it. But as with all elements of building your resilience, the more you do it, the easier and more automatic it becomes. From here you can start to look for patterns in what stimuli trigger a less than resilient reaction. Once pinpointed, you can change that relatively automatic reflex reaction, into a much more considered and measured, rational response. You retain control, gain insight into your triggers and reactions, and modify your contributions to future experiences accordingly.

Another way to control your brain is to try to keep it in the present. That's not to say that you shouldn't reminisce on the past or look forward to and plan for the future. But those events in the past cannot be changed, and the ones in the future can't be accurately predicted. It is therefore much wiser to pay attention closely to the only moment you have power over, and that moment is now.

Perhaps the most empowering knowledge to all difficult experiences, is the appreciation that all feelings, no matter how painful or intense, are only temporary. Even if the circumstance or challenge is permanent, the feeling is not. And with that knowledge comes the reassurance that better times are around the corner. We may need to remind ourselves of this regularly, to retain the fortitude to keep going. Just as one day in the past we felt wonderful and it sadly changed, so too this less desirable feeling will change one day and again we will be basking in the glow of warmth and positivity.

Nurture your Environment

Life is not a solo sport. We all need support sometimes. In fact, even if we don't need to call on our support networks, just knowing they're there is invaluable to our courage and confidence to press ahead. The people around you should be encouraging, kind and supportive of your goals and ambitions. They may equally provide effective challenge to help you. The aim is for a body of support, ready to help lift you up and spur you on. If there are people in your life who seem to do the opposite, it may be time to question their intentions and perhaps assess the value of the time you invest with them. If anyone consistently weakens your coping abilities rather than strengthens them, explore the value you are receiving (and possibly contributing) to the relationship.

As much as the people in our lives are enormously influential, so is our physical environment. Look around and appraise your surroundings. Do they make you feel good? Are there quick and easy fixes that would help you feel more comfortable? It may be that clearing some clutter would not just physically free up some space but help your frame of mind too. You are the master of your destiny and tiny incremental benefits can be found in every area of our life, to build your feel-good factor, positivity and ultimately, resilience.

Strengthen your Body to Sharpen your Mind

Your body and brain are inextricably linked.

"The brain takes its energy from the food that we eat and oxygen that we breathe …" (Scarlett, 2016).

As such, the way in which we care for our bodies is instrumental to our ability to perform effectively, and especially when confronted with challenges. Eat fresh, nutrient packed food to fuel yourself. Hydrate. The saying now goes that "sitting is the new smoking", due to our often damaging, sedentary lifestyles. Move. You do not have to go to the gym, just move your body with the purpose of developing strength, circulating oxygen and raising your pulse rate to build that all important heart muscle.

Carefully control your intake of substances known to be harmful including the numerous chemicals produced from smoking cigarettes. Limit alcohol intake to prevent descending into situations which may be risky to both your physical and mental wellbeing. Everything you do in this vein, not only provides protective factors against heart disease and some cancers, but also support a healthy mind. What's good for the heart is good for the head and that is good for positivity and resilience!

There are also countless ways in which you can use your body to change your frame of mind and very quickly. There is no one-size-fits-all, but whether you choose to dance around the kitchen to your favourite uplifting song, engage in deep breathing exercises, meditations, yoga, mindfulness or body scans, to create a pause and a moment of calm, if you change your physiology, you can change your mind to a more positive disposition. Try it right now. Quickly scan your body from toes to top. Spot where you are holding tension, where you're hunched, or muscles feel tense. Notice what state of mind or feelings you are experiencing at the same time. When you've finished, simply move yourself to a position which fosters greater relaxation, energy or comfort, whatever it is you need. Shake it out, move around and feel your mood change, in an instant. Repeat, regularly, every day.

Your Door to a Purposeful, Positive and Resilient Future

So, where do you go from here. Well, acknowledge that nothing changes unless your beliefs, thoughts and behaviours do. You are the catalyst and the beneficiary of every action you implement towards greater resilience.

The actions suggested in this book can help you to become a more resilient person. Being more resilient will result in suggested actions feeling much easier, and so the cycle continues. You may well have noticed by now that there is a theme here, that potential is everywhere. Small positive changes can accumulate to great personal advancement, if you are willing to seek out the opportunities around you.

Now come the tough questions. Ask yourself whether you are putting yourself under the right amount of challenge to build your resilience muscle. This should not be traumatic, driving you to such lengths that you eventually retreat from ever pushing your boundaries again. Ask yourself "what's the worst that could happen?" If the answer isn't so bad and you could live comfortably with the consequences, what have you got to lose? You will need to become comfortable with the uncomfortable to make progress. You don't need to get comfortable with the dangerous, however. It's good to take small and steady steps and just imagine how much bigger your comfort zone could be in a year from now, if in each week ahead, you were able to extend your "… ability to withstand adverse events and stressful situations without developing physical or emotional symptoms, by actively and positively coping with stress" (Stein & Book, 2011).

There are two questions you need to ask yourself now as you embark on your pursuit towards a more resilient life. The first is how confident do you feel, on a scale of 1 to 10, about your ability to become more resilient, with 1 being no confidence at all and 10 being supremely confident. If you score yourself anything less than a 10, you may be underestimating yourself. Take it from someone who knows, resilience might just be the greatest gift you ever present yourself. I challenge you to find three good reasons not to put into practice, strategies that can take you to a more resilient life. I'll be amazed if you can find just one.

The second is to ask yourself how important it is to you, that you become more resilient on the same scale of 1 to 10. Here is where your success will likely be determined. If the importance is high, you now have everything you need to go out and face life's challenges with zeal and positivity, assured of success. If you score low, it would be a great time to ask yourself why you would choose to proceed on your road trip through life without great shock absorbers. Only you have the answer.

If we have learnt anything from the challenges that 2020 has thrown at us already, it's that at some point, our road trip through life, will almost certainly be disrupted again. When it is, I anticipate that we'll leave the road and hit the sea. We'll all embark on the same boat on our voyage to our brave new world. Once aboard, some of us will have the benefit of having taught ourselves to swim. Some will have had the foresight to identify how to access the flotation devices. And the really determined among us will have worked diligently, to ensure we know how to launch and navigate the life rafts.

I plan to be among the final group and to make it smoothly to dry land, bringing as many people with me as I can. I really look forward to seeing you there.

For a free resilience audit, to help identify ways in which you can build your resilience muscle further, please visit www.wellbeingts.co.uk

About the Author

Helen Lawson is a freelance workplace wellbeing specialist, trainer, and speaker with a background spanning business, education, and health. She is passionate about supporting individuals to develop the skills to lead happier, healthier, and more fulfilling lives. Her focus on approaches which build confidence and competence, provide building blocks for a more positive future. She is also committed to helping businesses create and implement wellbeing strategies, which prioritise a supported workforce full of potential, and improved business efficiency and profitability.

Contact Details

Website	www.wellbeingts.co.uk
LinkedIn	www.linkedin.com/in/helen-lawson-educator
Facebook	https://www.facebook.com/wellbeingts/
Twitter	@WellbeingTS
Instagram	wellbeingtrainingsolutions

References

Covey, S. R., 2015. *The Seven Habits of Highly Effective People, iBookstore Special Video Edition,* Miami: FranklinCovey Co..

Grant, H., 2011. *Harvard Business Review.* [Online]
Available at: https://hbr.org/2011/05/be-an-optimist-without-being-a
[Accessed 14 May 2020].

Jay, M., 2018. *IDEAS.TED.COM.* [Online]
Available at: https://ideas.ted.com/8-tips-to-help-you-become-more-resilient/
[Accessed 14 May 2020].

Joseph, A., 2009. *Cognitive Behavioural Therapy.* 1st ed. Chichester: Capstone Publishing Ltd..

Marmer, S., 2018. *You Tube, PragerU.* [Online]
Available at: https://www.youtube.com/watch?time_continue=3&v=fPMqMJMiBiA&feature=emb_title
[Accessed 14 May 2020].

Rhimes, S., 2015. *SuperSoul Sunday, Life's Big Questions, Season 6, Episode 624* [Interview] (15 November 2015).

Scarlett, H., 2016. *Neuroscience for Organiszational Change.* 1st ed. London: Kogan Page Lmited.

Stein, S. J. & Book, H. E., 2011. *The EQ Edge, Emotional Intelligence and Your Success.* 3rd ed. s.l.:Jossey-Bass, A Wiley Imprint.

Finding balance in an unbalanced world
by Tracey Allport

Human beings are amazingly adaptable, but it can take time for us to adjust to change and situations which we have no control over, especially when they have been thrust upon us without prior warning, as there is little time for preparation.

We may start to adjust to our new normal and then the goal posts can change again. Different demands are placed upon us and how we respond will depend upon the resources that we have to manage or the many thoughts that we have and how we manage them.

Extraordinary events can elicit psychological and physical feelings which we may not have experienced in this way before.

These internal feelings can be defined as responses to stress, stressful situations or stressful events.

Understanding the stress response and its effects, with some easy to use strategies, can help us regain our homeostasis more readily.

What is stress?

The Dictionary defines stress as:

> "Stress is a state of mental or emotional strain, or tension, resulting from adverse or demanding circumstances."

Shiel (2018) defines stress as:

> "In a medical or biological context stress is a physical, mental, or emotional factor that causes bodily or mental tension. Stresses can be external (from the environment, psychological, or social situations) or internal (illness, or from a medical procedure)."

Stress can initiate the fight, flight or freeze response, which is a complex reaction of the neurologic and endocrinologic systems. In the days when we had to hunt and gather, hormones would have been released, to prepare us to run away, or fight the grizzly bear that was about to attack us. Sadly, in modern day times, our challenges are completely different, but our bodies respond in the same physiological way.

My clients come to me with physical tension somewhere in their body; often it's the shoulders, but not exclusively! They most often aren't even aware that the stressors of life are now creating physical issues for them, as a signal that they need to stop and take notice! What they do notice is that they have a physical pain and would like to be free of it. There is usually a much bigger picture, that unfolds through further discussion.

We have forgotten the art of tuning into our minds and bodies and have lost the ability to be self-aware, because frankly there are far too many things occupying our time and our minds.

Our brains are powerful organs and if we don't listen to signals, when we feel a bit 'off' and just keep ploughing on regardless (which is most often the case), then it will manifest itself somehow, in a way that we have no choice for us to stop and take notice. Migraine is a classic example of us having no choice but to stop and rest in a dark room to recover. I often hear my clients say, "But I just don't have time for this headache right now".

Imagine that you are driving your car and you veer off from your lane, onto the rumble strip and your car and whole body vibrates. Your awareness changes and you take notice that your car isn't where it is meant to be, as driving shouldn't feel like this, so you turn your steering wheel to get back into your lane!

Now, transfer this analogy to when you feel stressed. Your body is giving you signals that something is 'off'; it just doesn't feel right and you know that you are out of your lane and you need to get back on track! At what point do you stop, listen and change your direction?

So what happens when we are stressed?

Stress isn't necessarily a bad thing per se.

If we have no stress how would we feel? Bored, unmotivated, de-energised?

Healthy stress is termed 'Eustress' (Hans Selye 1975). He defined eustress, as stress that is healthy, or gives one a feeling of fulfilment, or other positive feelings. Performance increases with the right amount of eustress and declines with too much distress.

This is because a small amount of cortisol (stress hormone) improves our brain function, allowing us to function better in stressful situations e.g. we all recognise that feeling of a looming work deadline, that spurs us on to get it finished on time (or writing a chapter for a book!).

So, fundamentally achieving the right balance is key!

Which situations are likely to lead to feelings of stress?

These are termed stressors and they will be different for everyone. They can be external or internal in nature.

Take a moment to think about the stressors that you are currently exposed to?

Examples of common stressors may include:

- A change or loss of employment
- Lack of time
- Conflicts at home, work or in relationships
- Grief
- Illness
- Taking on too much
- Unhealthy lifestyle
- Major life changes
- Not taking time for self-care
- Over-thinking

We all react to individual stressors in different ways and this will vary according to the resources that we have available to us to cope.

Simply, if there is an imbalance between the demands being placed upon us and the resources that we have to manage them, our levels of stress will increase.

When our resources are outweighed by the demands of our life, we will perceive them as stressful and feel in a state of distress, because we are unbalanced.

Examples of Potential Demands V Resources

Demands

- The emotional, physical, financial, social demands of everyday life
- Adjustment to new situations e.g. work issues; unemployment, new job
- Lack of income
- Illness or pain
- Separation or divorce
- Birth of a baby
- Children leaving home
- Death of a loved one
- Our attitudes and expectations in relation to ourselves and others
- Lack of time
- Taking on too much/Not being able to say 'No'
- Separation from family or friends
- Care-giving
- Lack of control

Resources

- Physical health
- Money
- Skills and past experiences
- Flexibility and adaptability
- Aspirations and motivation

- Acceptance
- Strategies
- Attitudes, values and beliefs
- Emotional regulation
- Cognitive capacity
- Social support
- Communication networks
- Community
- Access to transport
- Spirituality/Faith
- Creativity
- Ability to relax

You may find it helpful to gain some perspective, by making a list of the demands that you currently have upon you and your available resources, both externally and intrinsically.

How do we know when we feel stressed?

Stress may present itself in a variety of ways and it can be different for each individual.

Some of the symptoms may include the following;

- Restlessness
- Memory problems
- Immune system reduction
- Constipation or diarrhoea/bowel problems
- Eating disorders or weight gain/loss

- Erectile dysfunction/loss of libido/reproductive problems
- Sweaty palms
- Heart palpitations
- Poor concentration
- Brain fog
- Shallow breathing
- Ulcers
- Worry, rumination, over-thinking
- Self-absorption
- Poor sleep
- Aches and pains/muscular tension (usually in the absence of injury)
- Skin problems, such as eczema or psoriasis

It is important to minimise stress levels to prevent chronic stress and to avoid long term illnesses, such as anxiety, burnout, depression, high blood pressure and irritable bowel syndrome. Chronic stress also promotes emotional inflexibility, drains our vitality and increases aging.

There is however some good news!

It is actually physiologically impossible to be stressed and relaxed at the same time, as the two responses are triggered by two separate parts of the nervous system (the sympathetic and parasympathetic systems). Physiologically they cannot work simultaneously.

Another positive point:

> It is possible to learn to activate your relaxation response and there are many ways to do so.

What happens when we are relaxed?

The relaxation response triggers changes in the body's systems; respiratory, circulatory, digestive, nervous and muscular systems.

- Decreased blood pressure
- Decreased cardiac input
- Increased energy conservation
- Decreased breathing rate
- Decreased muscular tension
- Decreased body metabolism
- Decreased oxygen consumption
- Increased blood clotting time
- Decreased heart rate
- Increased cognitive ability
- Increased emotional regulation
- Improvements in thinking and decision making
- Changes in brainwave patterns
- Increased feel good hormones

Give a few minutes thought to how you feel when you are in a relaxed state. Make a note of the physical and emotional signs that you become aware of.

How can we manage our demands and resources?

We know first-hand the demands that we experience on a daily basis are wide, varied and change from day to day; they are also unique to each individual.

As an Occupational Therapist we help our clients to consider the demands that they are managing and help them to readdress the balance.

We term this occupational balance.

Blackman (2004) proposes that it is "a relative state, recognisable by a happy or pleasant integration of life activities and demands"

The key areas of Occupational Balance

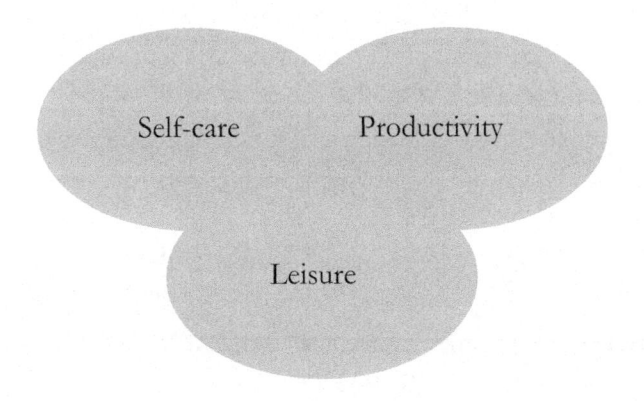

Self-care   Productivity

Leisure

Achieving balance in the 3 main key areas, of self-care (including rest), productivity and leisure is fundamental to our well-being.

It theorises that there should be harmony between the environment and the person and that it needs to be dynamic, transient and always changing, to accommodate different stages and times in our lives. Occupational balance is individualised and subjective, formed through interaction of internal and external elements related to the person, family, society and the environment.

Internal factors are related to a person's values, roles, identity, priorities, insight, capacity, importance, view and attitudes to life, future goals, ambitions and wants, spiritual beliefs/religion, choice, decisions, expectations and health/diagnosis.

External factors are related to family upbringing, culture and society, norms, expectations, standards, professional culture, environmental opportunities, supports and resources.

Both internal and external factors constantly readjust between personal and societal elements to form the concept of occupational balance.

It is also important to note that occupation (an activity we perform everyday) needs to be purposeful, meaningful, have sufficient complexity and for us to have sufficient willingness or a want to engage in it.

Simply, occupational balance is a personal affair that requires constant review and adjustment, being sensitive to our own rhythm.

The problems arise when we allow an imbalance to continue and it starts to cause strain and symptoms of physical and psychological distress, leading to tiredness, exhaustion, lack of structure & routine, feeling unwell, lack of time and reduced fulfilment, negative thinking, feelings of hopelessness, impact on confidence and self-esteem, difficulties with acceptance and grieving.

Take a moment to consider the three key areas and the occupations (activities) that you carry out on a daily basis.

Self-care examples may include; sleep and rest, nutrition, bathing, showering, meditation/mindfulness, prayer, massage, asking for help, time for reflection, talking about how you feel, hugs, gratitude, decluttering etc

Productivity examples may include; work roles, volunteering, caring for loved ones, parenting, DIY, household chores, studying or training courses, school and play (for children).

Leisure examples may include; hobbies, time with friends and family, reading, spending time in nature, watching TV or films, dancing, singing, attending church, exercise and ensuring technology down time.

Write a list of your activities in the three areas self-care, productivity and leisure.

Self-care	Productivity	Leisure

Now take some time to answer the following questions, considering the balance of activities.

1. Does one area appear more weighted than another?
2. Are you happy with the weighting?
3. Which activities are the most important to you and why?
4. What do you think is stopping you from achieving balance?
5. What changes can you make right now to address the balance?
6. What changes can you make in the future?
7. Which areas do you think require some help for you to make changes?
8. What kind of help do you need?

Occupational balance should provide a sense of joy, achievement and pride, feeding into an overall sense of satisfaction and happiness.

How to achieve personal balance

Building self-responsibility is key to managing the ups and downs of life and becoming resilient. We have an intrinsic drive to carry on, pick ourselves up and move forward.

There are three key elements to building self-responsibility.

1. Knowledge: gaining knowledge about yourself will increase your awareness of any imbalance that you may be feeling. You can then arm yourself with tools that will empower you and provide information to guide your way forward, to a healthier balance.

2. Decision: now consider the situation or imbalance that requires change. What process or action might you need to take to readdress the imbalance?

3. Action: set some measurable and achievable goals to implement your decision; these can be short term and longer-term goals but ensure that you set a date to implement your action. This will build your confidence and courage as you achieve what you have set out to achieve.

Ideas for relaxation and stress reduction:

So now that you've been able to analyse your stress responses, demands/resources, occupational balance and identified what changes you can make, it may be helpful to consider some useful strategies to maintain your balance of daily activities.

Firstly, understand and accept that ups and downs of life, feelings of stress and anxiety are perfectly normal, so do not beat yourself up.

You can learn to reverse your stress response by becoming aware of your stressors and the triggers will assist you with this ability.

Stop, rest and reflect. A busy mind is a full mind, which means there is no capacity for flexible thinking, generating fresh ideas or creativity. We need to stop feeling like a mouse on its wheel!

Allow yourself to feel; tune in to what your mind and body are saying to you. You know your own body and what it needs; we have just become too busy to listen!

We need to meet ourselves where we are at; what I mean by that, is that we do not have to fight ourselves to change our feelings. That in itself can create an internal battle as we try to change what we are experiencing. Acknowledging and accepting our feelings, takes away the struggle and gives ourselves permission to experience the rich emotions of life. Of course, we want to feel happy and content, but in reality, life would be pretty colourless without a range of emotions. And remember that these emotions can be different each day or even within days.

A lot of my clients say they have problems relaxing; their minds are whirring at 150 miles per hour and they just cannot switch off. The reality is that all of our minds are constantly busy; we experience 60-90,000 thoughts per day! But we can choose whether to engage in the thoughts or not. You can actively choose to let them go.

We can allow those thoughts to just pass us by, like bubbles floating away or we can create internal stories and dialogues, getting caught up in the emotional content. It may take a little practice, either by setting a conscious intention to let things go or work with a CONTROL Practitioner who can help you to understand your limiting beliefs and change behaviours and patterns of thought, that you want to change, painlessly.

Consider your goals; are your thoughts and behaviours propelling you towards your goals or are they getting in your way? Meditation can also help to teach you to shift your focus away from the mind monkeys, onto your breath, body or an object. There are lots of different types of meditations available, with something to suit everybody. My approach to meditation practice is to make it functional, practical and accessible for everyone. Amazingly, only 3 minutes a day is required to rewire your brain and facilitate feelings of calm. A really practical meditation, that anyone can do, is simply to take a breath in through your nose, saying to yourself, "I am breathing in" and as you breath out slowly through your mouth say, "I am breathing out". This will shift your focus to your breath, away from your busy mind and it will physiologically calm you, by turning off the emotional centre of the brain (amygdala) and slowing your breathing, expanding the diaphragm and triggering the vagus nerve, which will bring about a sense of calm and relaxation.

Live in the present moment (mindfulness); "That is easier said than done", I hear you shout! But stress cannot live in the here and now. Stress is created by living in and ruminating on the past or worrying about the future. Try going for a walk and appreciate the sounds of the birds, the warmth of the sun on your face, the pressure of the ground through your feet and the sights of nature around you. You'll find that your mind focuses on your senses processing information, your appreciation creates joy and gratitude and it becomes impossible to focus on worries or concerns at the same time. They may try to come into your mind, just allow them to pass on by, as you maintain your focus on your senses instead.

Give yourself permission to take care of yourself. It is not self-indulgent, it is vital so you can then be available and perform your best, for your other priorities. If you are not functioning as the best version of you, how can you expect to support those around you?

Protect your relaxation time; schedule it into your diary, as it is vital to your health and well-being. This will help you to build positive resilience forming habits.

Ensure you manage your sleep routine and sleep hygiene habits. Sleep is your friend, it should not be considered a waste of time, nor used to catch up on jobs you feel that you should have done during the day. If your resources are in deficit you will suffer, so prepare yourself for any eventuality, that might occur, by having lots of fuel in your tank!

Here's a list of other ideas that you may like to explore:

- Massage therapy
- Aromatherapy
- Osteopathy
- The CONTROL System
- Self-hypnosis / Hypnotherapy
- Reflexology
- Talking therapies/CBT/Psychotherapy/Counselling/Coaching
- Meditation/Mindfulness practices
- Practice gratitude and seek out the positive
- Progressive muscular relaxation
- Breathing techniques
- Trigger words
- Anchoring

- Brain entrainment (binaural beats)
- Rag doll
- Guided imagery
- Body scan
- Healing sounds
- Moving your attention from head to heart focus
- Anchoring
- Positive statements (affirmations)
- Paraliminals (beyond the threshold of conscious processing)
- Yoga Nidra (Yogic sleep)
- Pilates or Yoga
- Exercise
- Walking in nature
- Being by the sea
- Eat a healthy balanced diet; avoid caffeine, alcohol and sugar
- Herbal or homeopathic remedies
- Drink black tea
- Avoid toxic people
- Avoid stressful situations where possible
- Put positive psychology into action
- Time management
- Fatigue management/pacing techniques
- Learn to say 'No'.
- Delegate
- Prayer

- Join a religious community
- Join a support group
- Nurture supportive relationships
- Accountability
- Laughter
- Chew gum (reduces cortisol levels)
- Sex, Hugs, positive touch
- Hang out with your pet
- Engage in purposeful meaningful activity e.g. gardening
- Creative activity e.g. art, knitting, drawing, colouring etc.
- Journaling, free writing or blogging
- Listen to music
- Singing
- Reduce screen time, access to social media or the news
- Ask for help

This is a long list and by no means can you, nor do you need to do everything!

Start with one thing that brings you joy and make it a positive and regular habit.

Initially it takes time to learn relaxation techniques. Bizarrely, it takes 21 days of worrying to facilitate a worrying mind and 66 days of engaging in a positive habit, to make it a healthy and consistent practice!

But with repetition new neural pathways are laid down, so that the relaxation response can be triggered when required and the effects are cumulative.

There are lots of free resources available via the internet or Apps. And there are many self-help books written on a variety of subjects. It helps to find one that resonates with you and you find pleasing; you're more likely to stick with something if you enjoy it.

The key is not to become overwhelmed. Reach out to a practitioner who specialises in stress management or any of the other techniques that have piqued your interest.

If you'd like further information about my services, to help with managing, stress, anxiety, overwhelm, burnout or low mood, or if you would like a free audio meditation 'managing thoughts', or a copy of a free meditation e-book, email tracey@moththerapies.co.uk

I would especially love to hear your feedback on this chapter and how it has helped you. Please email me directly, or via the contact form on my website.

About the Author

Tracey is a master of mind and body therapies, supporting women who experience stress, overwhelm, anxiety or burnout.

Having qualified as an Occupational Therapist, some 28 years ago and worked primarily in the fields of neurology, acquired brain injury and mental health, she went on to study coaching, remedial hypnosis, and complementary therapies, including massage, aromatherapy and meditation, to be able to provide comprehensive therapeutic interventions and breakthrough coaching conversations.

MOTH Therapies offers tailor made services to clients, who are proactive and want to be self-empowered to make changes, so that they feel in control of themselves again.

Based in her beautiful bespoke studio in Whitstable, for face to face connections, or virtually if you are further afield.

Contact details:

Website: www.moththerapies.co.uk
Facebook: www.facebook.com/moththerapies
Instagram: www.instagram.com/moth_therapies
Linkedin: Tracey (Reay) Allport
Email: tracey@moththerapies.co.uk

References:

Blackman, C. L. (2004) 'Occupational Balance; Exploring the relationships among daily occupations and their influence on well-being.', *Canadian Journal of Occupational Therapy*, 71(4), pp. 202-209.

Malia, K. (2012) *Brain Tree Training: Active relaxation training workshop*. Available at: https://www.braintreetraining.co.uk/UK_Gatwick_course_details.php?id=107 (Accessed: 09 May 2020).

Shiel, W.C. (2018) *Medical Definition of Stress*. Available at: https://www.medicinenet.com/script/main/art.asp?articlekey=20104 (Accessed: 10 May 2020).

Diet and Lifestyle Changes for Enhancing Energy, Balancing moods, Restful Sleep and A Robust Immune System

by Caroline Sherlock

2020 Lockdown has resulted in many people struggling; anxious about the future, feeling low and lethargic after spending time in isolation and afraid of a virus that we are unable to see nor seemingly do anything about.

But there are steps that we can take right now - very simple dietary and lifestyle changes that we can make to help us to feel better - to support our immune system, energy, moods and sleep. There are simple ways in which we can build resilience and optimise our health. There is no need to just 'wait' in fear of an attack by an invisible invader or to become afraid of going out until a vaccine arrives. These are factors that are beyond our control but empowering ourselves with the knowledge about how we can support our own immune system is a game changer. Nutritional strategies to support energy, moods, sleep and immune function are often missed in public health discussions yet evidence-based research is there in abundance. Eating well, drinking well and living well can make dramatic changes to our health are absolutely something that we can control.

There are simple solutions - changing what we eat and how we live to feel more energised, happier, optimistic and better rested. We are also able to influence how our immune systems respond to invaders and better equip them to deal more efficiently with invaders. A well-functioning immune system should operate silently preventing attacks from unseen bacteria and viruses, winning the attack and then repairing and healing almost without us even knowing about the battle. Good nutrition is paramount to this but during lockdown it really was the last thing people were thinking about. Pasta, refined flour, biscuits, ice cream and alcohol flew off the shelves and many have been comfort eating and drinking to cope with the lack of routine, isolation and fear and anxiety of the situation.

Yet if there was ever a time to reflect on our lifestyle, on our own individual stressors, on how resilient we are and how we may change that and the quality of foods that we put into our mouths, then this is it. How we feel and the robustness of our immune systems are directly related to how we nourish ourselves and the self-care and kindness that we show ourselves. This is a time for reflection, and hopefully change.

Understanding the factors that contribute towards low energy, fluctuating moods, poor sleep and an imbalanced immune system means looking at the root causes of these. This is what a functional medicine approach is. Understanding why – and then looking at the areas that we control – diet and lifestyle in order to change our health trajectory or outcome.

Let's begin with energy.

Enhancing Energy:

Low energy levels can have many causes, including a deficiency of essential nutrients required for energy production, including Vitamin B12 or iron. This is why ticking the box of a balanced diet is important in order to get the widest possible spread of nutrients. By balanced diet we mean a mix of protein (animal and vegetable), carbohydrates (wholegrains and a wide diversity of other plant foods), healthy fats (olive oil, cold-pressed seed oils, avocado, coconut, butter) and fluids (ideally water). If your energy is low, it is worth asking your doctor to run a few blood tests including thyroid function.

Beyond this though, we know that stress and chronic inflammation are massive contributors to tiredness and fatigue. This is via activation of the HPA Axis (Hypothalamus Pituitary Adrenal) Axis – interlinking the hypothalamus, the pituitary and the adrenal glands in order to manage the body's initial response to stress. The end result of this activation is cortisol production. Cortisol is released as part of our 'fight or flight' response – it assumes we are running away from a threat – for example a lion. Cortisol releases glucose into the blood and reduces insulin production so that our muscles and brain are well-fuelled and we can run and think quickly. Cortisol is anti-inflammatory in case we are injured and shuts digestive processes down as it is unlikely (hopefully!) that we are eating when we are running.

However, once the stressor is gone – cortisol levels should return to normal. The issue is when our stress response is constantly turned on – or if we have underlying chronic systemic inflammation that is activating cortisol on a constant basis.[1] In terms of energy, cortisol impacts thyroid function (a symptom of low thyroid function is fatigue), sex hormone production (contributing for instance to menstrual irregularities) and eventually suppresses the immune system and disrupts sleep; when we are looking to support energy, maintaining a normal cortisol level is imperative.

Managing ongoing stressors and our response to those through lifestyle changes and reducing sources of chronic inflammation are therefore, prime targets in order to normalise cortisol function.

While we are addressing stress and inflammation, the quickest thing we can do to help reduce cortisol dysregulation and raise energy is by addressing our blood glucose balance.

Blood glucose is tightly regulated by the body to remain within a narrow band. This is in order for the brain to receive a constant supply of glucose, which is its main energy source. Blood sugar levels can rise too quickly when we are anxious, fearful, when we take stimulants including caffeine or when we eat processed, refined carbohydrates and carbohydrates that release their sugar very quickly. Examples of this would be a slice of toast, white rice, chocolate, biscuits, sugar itself - and soft drinks and juices. These flood our blood rapidly with sugar. Healthy foods can also do this such as a baked potato and many fruits including bananas and dried fruit. These foods are known as high Glycaemic Load (GL) foods. These healthy high GL foods are not inherently 'bad' but they do need to be eaten in combination with other foods to mitigate their fast release of sugar.

The impact of eating these foods is that the pancreas releases insulin to safely lower the level of sugar in the blood. High levels of sugar in the blood damages our cells and tissues, creating AGEs (Advanced Glycation End products), inflammation and activation of the immune system. The immune system is now diverted from its role of defence against invaders and is instead focused on repairing an inflammatory situation that we have in fact caused ourselves, using valuable antioxidants to do so.

Reducing glucose from a high level results in sugar levels plummeting and reaching a level that is too low - at this stage we experience a sudden dip in energy (much like the mid-afternoon or post-lunch slump), accompanied by a low mood and irritability. This is the body indicating to us that glucose levels need to come back up again. Our response here would be to comfort eat - reach for a bowl of cereal, a plate of pasta, a biscuit, bar of chocolate or glass of juice. These typically are high GL foods, so blood sugar rises rapidly and overshoots again.

If we choose not to eat to get sugar levels up, adrenaline and cortisol are released from the adrenal glands and the pancreas releases another hormone known as glucagon; sugar levels rise in this way. The cycle continues, the net result being that we feel like we are on an energy and mood rollercoaster, constantly triggering our immune system and activating systemic inflammation in the body.

We also now know that make up of our gut microbiome (all the microorganisms including bacteria, fungi and viruses) directly impacts our blood sugar response to the foods that we eat – in part due to how quickly they feed on the carbohydrate foods and release that sugar into the blood stream. But also, as they can be potent modulators of inflammation. Inflammation as we now know triggers cortisol and glucose production.[2]

When this cycle continues on an ongoing basis, not only are energy, moods and immunity impacted but insulin resistance can develop - contributing to metabolic syndrome and a pre-diabetic state. Type 2 Diabetes is when we become so resistant to insulin that sugar levels remain high. The sugar is essentially ringing the bell on the cell door to be let in, but the doorbell is being ignored.

The continual production of cortisol is also unhelpful; cortisol disrupts sleep, is an immune-suppressant and promotes storage of fats - resulting in abdominal adiposity (belly fat). This is not a good combination. We now feel worse as we're chronically inflamed and can't lose fat around the middle.

We know this combination of insulin resistance, obesity and impaired glucose tolerance have all been shown to be associated with inflammation.[3]

The great news is that there are some very simple solutions to support energy production and blood sugar balance:

Action Steps:

- Better manage stress and identify sources of chronic inflammation – this is instrumental in supporting blood glucose and cortisol levels.
- Get restful sleep to help raise energy
- Make simple dietary changes beginning with a reduction of high GL foods (processed, refined foods), sugary snacks and in particular soft drinks - including colas (diet versions have the same impact as sugary versions due to their impact on the gut microbiome) and juices
- Follow a Rainbow Diet. This is a diet with an absolute minimum of seven differently coloured plant foods per day. This raises fibre and lowers the impact of high sugar foods, nourishes the gut microbiome (which helps to control blood sugar levels)[2] and adds antioxidants to help reduce inflammation.
- Eat a small amount of protein with every meal and snack. In practice this means eating a banana alongside a handful of nuts, a smaller sized baked potato with a topping of bean or meat chilli and salad, or dates stuffed with peanut butter. Protein sources can be animal or vegetable - eggs, poultry, meat, fish, tofu, beans, lentils, chickpeas, nuts and seeds are all good sources. It is the protein that makes a difference to the overall GL of the meal or snack.

A beneficial by-product of supporting energy and blood sugar regulation is that moods should also improve! But there are also additional pathways we can support to impact how happy we are, how motivated and how relaxed we feel.

Balancing Moods

Working on how we manage stress is crucial, especially if we have little control at this moment over the actual stressful situation itself – whether that is isolation, personal problems, financial or job worries.

But there are also very many other practical things that can be done to help support moods by understanding some of the root causes of why we feel the way we do.

Following the action steps to balance blood sugar is the first change.

An additional benefit of this is that by making sure that you have a small amount of protein with each meal you will also be ensuring a regular intake of amino acids necessary for your body to make the neurotransmitters it needs. These are chemical messengers including adrenaline, noradrenaline, serotonin, dopamine and GABA (Gamma aminobutyric acid) - and our ability to make and break them down is influenced by our genetics and by nutrition. Some people may need a little more help than others.

Serotonin is the 'feel good' or 'happy' neurotransmitter and relies on an amino acid called tryptophan for its production. Stress and disrupted blood sugar raise cortisol. Cortisol and inflammation both divert tryptophan away from serotonin synthesis meaning that we may produce less serotonin. This is an issue because serotonin not only makes us feel good but is converted to our sleep hormone melatonin. Ensuring high enough levels of nutrients including Vitamins B6, B12 and folate, Vitamin D, iron, magnesium and zinc - as well as consuming cruciferous (broccoli, brussels sprouts, cabbage, cauliflower, kale, mustard rocket, watercress), vegetables can help to push tryptophan down the serotonin pathway rather than being diverted.

Over 80% of serotonin is produced in the gut; the gut is connected to the brain via the vagal nerve, so our moods are also closely connected to the health of our gut. Ensuring the health of our gut as with blood sugar and energy regulation, is also impactful on our moods too.

Tyrosine is another important amino acid and is required for both thyroid hormone production (having a suboptimal thyroid function can contribute to lack of energy and low moods) and dopamine production. Dopamine is the 'motivational' neurotransmitter and can be helpful if feeling lethargic. Vitamin D, B vitamins including folate and Vitamin B6 can be helpful in supporting dopamine production from tyrosine. Although if dopamine levels are too high, this can contribute to feeling 'tired and wired' (particularly if we are producing excessive levels of adrenaline in response to stress). In this case nutrients to help break down dopamine can be really beneficial - particularly magnesium.

GABA is our relaxation neurotransmitter and helps us to chill. The nutrients magnesium, manganese, Vitamin B6 and zinc are helpful in making GABA. The amino acid l-theanine (found in green tea), and herbs valerian, chamomile, lemon balm, basil, oregano, sage, mint and rosemary can help to 'keep' GABA where it is.

Omega 3 Essential Fatty Acids, particularly EPA and DHA are an important component of a balanced mood diet. A low intake of the Omega 3 fats in particular may predispose some people to depression and anxiety and an obvious solution is to simply raise intake of these dietary fats.[4] Omega 3 fats help to support the cell membrane structure so that neurotransmitters, hormones, chemical messengers and nutrients can freely move in and out, they are vital for brain function and are potent triggers of anti-inflammatory pathways. These are found in oily fish such as SMASH fish (sardines, mackerel, anchovies, salmon and herring). They are also found in small amounts in pumpkin seeds, chia seeds, flaxseeds, hemp seeds and walnuts. So, if you are not eating oily fish – now may be the time to start or to consider supplements if you are vegetarian or vegan.

Action Steps:

- Continue to balance blood sugar levels
- Support the health of your gut by following a Rainbow Diet in order to feed our microbiome and to support serotonin production and 'positive' messages being fed to the brain via the Vagal nerve.
- Ensure enough protein is being eaten to make neurotransmitters - and that you chew well to support digestion of the protein into amino acids.
- Add Essential Fatty Acids to your diet by eating two portions of SMASH fish each week (Sardines, Mackerel, Anchovies, Salmon, Herring)
- Ensure a diverse diet to include adequate intake of B vitamins, magnesium, manganese, zinc and Vitamin B6 for serotonin synthesis. Magnesium is particularly important to help 'switch off' and can be found in wholegrains, nuts, seeds and green vegetables.
- Find out your Vitamin D levels with a Vitamin D test. Supplement Vitamin D to an appropriate level if your levels

are suboptimal and ensure regular exposure to the sun each day. This helps to support neurotransmitter production

- To promote relaxing GABA, include calming teas such as chamomile and lemon balm (young plants can be found cheaply in garden centres and is the easiest way to make fresh lemon balm tea) and use herbs in cooking as much as possible
- Drink green tea three to four times a day for l-theanine to help promote GABA

Balancing blood sugar, energy and moods have a benefit on our immunity just by themselves. But there is much more we are able to do to support our own individual immune systems.

A Robust Immune System

A robust immune system is so important and yet we give it little thought normally, perhaps eating a few more oranges if we feel like a cold is coming. Yet if our immune system works well, we are able to effectively prevent infection, mount appropriate immune activity when we are infected and then turn the inflammation off when it has done its job. We shouldn't even be aware this process is happening inside us if all is going to plan.

Yet chronic inflammation and stress mean that many people have ongoing disruption to this process – with an imbalance resulting in an ineffective immune system, an immune system that is always 'switched on' or one that has progressed to autoimmunity.

Our immune system is complex, with many different elements - organs, cells and cytokines (chemical messengers) involved. The immune system has two prime aims - to defend us from invaders and to repair from injury. There are two main arms of the immune system and both need to work in balance together. The Innate Immune system is our immediate response and is the first line of defence against invading microorganisms. The second part is known as the adaptive immune system and is focused largely on antibody production – taking 3-5 days before becoming fully operational. Both parts need to behave appropriately in order to be effective.

Inflammatory cytokines (messengers) are generated as part of the immune system switching on - but it is important that these are turned off when appropriate to avoid a cytokine storm - basically unregulated inflammation that can not switch off. If our immune system does not switch off or cannot deal appropriately with an invader – or is over-stimulated – it is an issue!

Our diet and lifestyle choices can profoundly influence how well the immune system works and yet nutritional support is still not viewed as a key intervention despite the evidence-based research that exists. It is widely acknowledged that vitamins and minerals including Vitamins A, B6, B12, C, D, E, folate and zinc, iron, selenium, magnesium and copper, play important and complementary roles in supporting both the innate and adaptive immune systems. Deficiencies or suboptimal status in micronutrients negatively affect immune function and can decrease resistance to infections.[5]

Other essential nutrients such as Omega 3 fats, phytonutrients including quercetin, bromelain, curcumin, glutathione, EGCG (from green tea) and NAC have also been shown to take supportive roles in immune regulation.[3]

It therefore is possible for us to change our health trajectory by supporting the immune system via dietary modifications and raising intake of specific nutrients. In short, we are able to influence how well our immune system performs when challenged, how well we deal with an infection, and how well we recover from that by addressing our diet and lifestyle.

Improvements in diet are strongly associated with reductions in inflammation but it is also important to get rid of inflammation that does not have a purpose - that caused by poor food and lifestyle choices that generate blood sugar dysregulation, gut disruption and inflammation.

We need to step back and let the immune system do what it should - rather than get mis-directed coping with dietary and lifestyle derived inflammation.

The starting area of focus for immune support is the gut. Over 70% of the immune system is located in the gut and it is therefore entirely logical that supporting gut health, particularly by nourishing the gut microbiome, (all the flora that live in the gut - which outnumber the entire number of cells we have in our body) supports our immune status.

Dysregulation of the gut microbiome bacteria has been shown to be a source of systemic inflammation.[2] An unhealthy gut has repeatedly been linked with inflammation, obesity, dysregulation of blood sugar and insulin - and an impaired immune response as a direct result of this. But there are simple ways to turn this around by raising intake of prebiotic foods (Rainbow Diet and plant foods) that stimulate 'good' gut bacteria that contribute towards a healthy microbiome. Raising intake of plant foods also ensures a healthy supply of Short Chain Fatty Acids which provide the all-important energy for the cells in the gut. Getting out into the garden and working with the soil is another great way to support the gut microbiome – it's also good for Vitamin D levels, is great for the soul and exercise too! In order to support our immune status - we must start with the gut.

Specific micronutrients are particularly important for our immunity. Vitamin C is probably the most well-known nutrient for immunity and plays many varied roles in impacting how we react to pathogens and viruses across both the innate and adaptive immune system. It is one of the top immune supportive nutrients for good reason.

A deficiency of Vitamin C contributes to a lowered immune system and raised susceptibility to infections. When inflammation exists (including damage by dysregulated blood glucose levels, and by our reaction to stress as well as fighting off microbes or repairing from injury) there is a raised demand for Vitamin C in the body. Vitamin C reduces the duration and severity of the common cold[6] and upper respiratory tract infections through a wide range of mechanisms, helping the immune system to kill viruses. It has also been shown that people who are deficient in Vitamin C are susceptible to severe respiratory infections such as pneumonia.[5]

Laboratory research indicates that sugar suppresses white blood cells in the immune system and emerging studies suggest that sugar also competes with Vitamin C to enter cells.[7] This therefore would reinforce that eating a high sugar diet - or a high carbohydrate, refined diet, is detrimental, rather than beneficial to the immune system particularly at times of infection. If you want your immune system to function well, ditch the sugary drinks, sweets and biscuits.

Vitamin D is another crucial nutrient for immune support, vital for activating our immune defences on so many different levels. The main source of Vitamin D is not food, but sunlight. Genetic differences, ethnicity, age, sunscreens (including in makeup) and a lack of outdoor time - even if the sun is out - simply mean that many people are deficient in Vitamin D. This is a huge issue for immunity and is one reason why influenza and other respiratory viruses peak over winter, when Vitamin D levels are lower.

Many immune cells have Vitamin D receptors, meaning that Vitamin D helps them to work. It activates and enhances immune system cells that destroy invading viruses, supports both sides of the immune system (killing pathogens but also generating antibodies) and regulates the production of inflammatory cytokines - switching off the inflammatory process when it is time.[3] Vitamin D deficiency also increases the risk for respiratory infection with observational studies showing an association between low vitamin D and susceptibility to acute respiratory tract infections.[8]

The best way to establish whether a Vitamin D supplement is of benefit is to test your levels through your doctor or a simple home finger-prick test.

Vitamin A is an often-overlooked vitamin. It is found in animal foods – primarily liver and dairy foods in the form that the body can readily use. We normally think of Vitamin A as beta-carotene for example in carrots or spinach, but this is in fact the Vitamin A precursor, and must be converted in the body to Vitamin A. However, some people have a relatively common genetic polymorphism whereby they are unable to efficiently convert beta-carotene into Vitamin A. This means that more attention to a Rainbow Diet and animal forms of Vitamin A should be considered as a dietary change.

Vitamin A is of huge importance to our immunity. It works very closely with Vitamin D helping to regulate immune function and is required for our mucosal barriers - put simply, the barriers lining the gastrointestinal tract, our lungs and nasal passages – anywhere where pathogens may enter the body. A Vitamin A deficiency, which is common worldwide, raises inflammation and imbalances our immune system, impairs the mucosal barrier integrity particularly in the respiratory and gastrointestinal tracts and raises the risk of asthma and allergies.[3] So, there is very good reason to pay attention to Vitamin A.

Zinc is another absolutely vital nutrient for the immune system, working closely with Vitamin C. Zinc helps to suppress viral replication by transferring into the cell, reduces the duration of the common cold[9] and turns off an overactive immune system. Zinc deficiency negatively impacts our immune defences resulting in increased risk of inflammation.[10] Some people require more zinc than others, particularly the elderly due to both low dietary intake and lower stomach acid levels. A symptom of zinc deficiency is loss of smell and taste which is consistent with that which is reported by those with a viral infection. [3] Good food sources of zinc include red meat, shellfish, fish, legumes (chickpeas, lentils and beans), nuts, seeds and eggs.

Quercetin is a phytonutrient found in foods such as apples, red onions, asparagus. It plays a very useful role in helping the immune system on many levels but particularly in reducing the inflammatory compound histamine and in reducing viral load, replication and lung inflammation.[11] Quercetin also plays an important role in helping zinc to cross the cell membranes - so helping zinc be more efficient in its role in the immune response.[3]

Glutathione is the body's master antioxidant with a crucial role in immune system regulation and support, along with its precursor, NAC (N-acetyl cysteine). Both glutathione and NAC have been used to support respiratory tract immunity, normalisation of inflammation and reduction of excessive mucous secretion in the body.[12] Vitamins C, Vitamin E and selenium help to support glutathione and so ensuring an adequate intake of each of these is important. Vitamin E also has been shown to modulate the immune system, particularly around upper respiratory tract infections.[13] Selenium also deserves a standalone place as an immune supportive nutrient in its own right.

Some people have a genetic polymorphism meaning that they are unable to produce glutathione effectively and these people may require more glutathione and antioxidant support. Glutathione and NAC may both be supplemented but eating allium rich food (onions, leeks, garlic) and cruciferous vegetables (broccoli, brussels sprouts, cabbage, cauliflower, kale, mustard rocket, watercress) help to support levels.

Omega 3 fats, particularly EPA and DHA from oily fish are potent modulators of inflammation in the body, helping to promote anti-inflammatory pathways.[5] As such they are an important component of an immune protocol.

Other phytonutrients that are extremely helpful in supporting immune function include:

- Curcumin (a component of turmeric) has multiple, broad spectrum anti-inflammatory and antimicrobial properties [14]
- Bromelain (found in pineapple) modulates both sides of the immune system and is particularly useful for conditions where there is increased mucus production and inflammation, including asthma, bronchitis and sinusitis[15]
- Beta-glucans (found in mushrooms) have been shown to possess very potent immunomodulatory effects, supporting the innate and adaptive immune system and supporting gut immunity, particularly Asian mushrooms including shiitake and reishi [16]
- Epigallocatechin-3-gallate (EGCG) and l-theanine (in green tea) have both been shown to reduce viral replication and influenza severity [17]

- Resveratrol (found in red grape skins and red wine) also demonstrates anti-viral activity particularly with respiratory infection [18]

It is clear there is an abundance of dietary changes and foods that we can include to support our immune systems. To raise your intake of immune supportive nutrients, focus on the following.

Action Steps:

- Eat a Rainbow Diet to support intake of a broad spread of nutrients and antioxidants that support the immune system
- Support the gut microbiome by consuming prebiotic foods (Rainbow Diet) and probiotic foods such as live yogurt, kefir, kombucha, olives, sauerkraut
- Within the Rainbow diet focus on cruciferous (broccoli, brussels sprouts, cabbage, cauliflower, kale, mustard rocket, watercress) and allium (garlic, onion, leeks) vegetables, plus pineapple, turmeric, apples, asparagus, red grapes and mushrooms
- Eat liver and butter for Vitamin A
- Eat red meat, nuts, seeds, fish and shellfish for zinc
- Eat oily (SMASH) fish twice a week for Omega 3 fats
- Drink green tea for l-theanine and EGCG (3-5 cups per day)
- Test your Vitamin D levels and get outside as much as possible
- Balance your blood sugar, stress and sources of chronic inflammation to reduce extra, unnecessary immune system activation

Sleep is the final area that many people struggle with but again, there are dietary and lifestyle changes that we can make to sleep soundly.

Restful Sleep:

It is often easier said than done particularly when feeling anxious, but supporting restful sleep is crucial to our health. At its most basic a lack of sleep contributes to fatigue - and poor food choices the next day.

Sleep enhances our immune defences, including anti-viral protection. Signals from immune cells also promote sleep.[19] The immune system and our sleep patterns have a bi-directional relationship[20] in that disrupted sleep raises cortisol levels (and vice versa - raised cortisol levels disrupt sleep) which is why stress reduction, inflammation reduction and blood sugar management are so crucial and interlinked with restful sleep.

Sleep is the time when we re-energise, detoxify and repair. Disrupted sleep has been linked to cognitive issues including a lack of consolidation of short-term memories as well as a lack of clearing of waste material from the brain and has been linked in research to a raised risk of Alzheimer's Disease and dementia. [21]

Alongside a healthy sleep routine, balancing blood sugar is key to a good night's sleep and is a relatively easy solution. If that does not yield benefits, then there are some other ways in which we can support sleep. Promoting the serotonin pathway is one of these ways as melatonin (our sleep hormone) is derived from serotonin. Other ways to support melatonin production include simple lifestyle measures such as exposure to sunlight in the middle of the day and dimming the lights in the evening to signal to the body it is time to sleep. Melatonin is also a potent antioxidant and anti-inflammatory and is of particular interest in relation to anti-viral activity. [22]

Melatonin is found in many plant foods but particularly in Montmorency tart cherries, which can be bought as a juice. In order to support sleep, promoting GABA pathways for relaxation can also be very helpful, in addition to raising intake of magnesium and the amino acid glycine.

Action:

- Balance blood sugar levels (and reduce stress and chronic inflammation!) to avoid waking in the night with low blood sugar and to avoid high cortisol levels which disrupt sleep.
- Avoid caffeine after lunch, and entirely if you are sensitive. This includes colas, chocolate, tea and coffee
- Avoid alcohol before bed in order to avoid disrupted sleep
- Enjoy healthy calming teas and include green tea through the day for l-theanine (GABA)
- Raise intake of magnesium (wholegrains, green leafy vegetables, nuts and seeds)
- Experiment with a tryptophan rich snack before bed to support serotonin - such as a small banana with nut butter or oat cake and follow recommendations for serotonin pathway support
- Ensure your last fluid intake is at least 2 hours before bed to avoid night-time urination
- Find a healthy sleep routine and stick to it if it works!

Reviewing the contributory factors to low energy, fluctuating moods, poor sleep and an imbalanced immune system means we able to intervene and change our health path. We are able to address these health symptoms with evidence backed, relatively simple dietary and lifestyle changes. Many of the recommendations overlap due to the common linkage of gut disruption and chronic inflammation driving dysregulation and imbalance. At its most basic, this comes down to selecting foods that are anti-inflammatory in nature while avoiding foods that are proinflammatory – following a Rainbow diet, with whole plant-based foods rich in phytonutrients, adding healthy fats and proteins to achieve a stable blood glucose response. [23]

There are so many ways to optimise our wellbeing and immune resilience going forward that are entirely in our control, should we choose to act on them. Now is a time for reflection.

To receive more information on the Rainbow Diet including a PDF download please go to https://mailchi.mp/23ad573b8864/rainbow-fruits-and-vegetables-guide

To book an Immune Support Consultation with the Eat Drink Live Well Clinic please go to https://www.eatdrinklivewell.com/consultations/

Contact sayhello@eatdrinklivewell.com for a Vitamin D Test Kit or for information on our 12 week online programme The Eat Drink Live Well Method: Connecting the Dots to your Health.

About the Author

Caroline Sherlock, BA(ss), Dip ION, IFMCP, MBANT, CNHC
Registered Nutritional Therapist
Institute for Functional Medicine, Certified Practitioner

Caroline Sherlock is co-founder of the Eat Drink Live Well Clinic and is a Registered Nutritional Therapist and Institute for Functional Medicine Certified Practitioner.

Caroline graduated with distinction from the Institute for Optimum Nutrition in 2005. She most recently trained with the Institute for Functional Medicine in the USA and in 2017 became one of the first UK-based IFM Certified Practitioners.

In clinic, Caroline works with highly motivated individuals who want to understand and address the root cause of their symptoms. Clients typically have multiple complex, chronic health symptoms or diagnoses and may have already seen many different practitioners. Through the Eat Drink Live Well Clinic, Caroline also runs online programmes, gives talks, writes health articles and mentors other nutritionists who are just starting their careers.

Caroline can be contacted at:

caroline@eatdrinklivewell.com
Tel +44 7786 405758
www.eatdrinklivewell.com

References

Hannibal, K. and Bishop, M., 2014. Chronic Stress, Cortisol Dysfunction, and Pain: A Psychoneuroendocrine Rationale for Stress Management in Pain Rehabilitation. *Physical Therapy*, 94(12), pp.1816-1825.

Blander, J., Longman, R., Iliev, I., Sonnenberg, G. and Artis, D., 2017. Regulation of inflammation by microbiota interactions with the host. *Nature Immunology*, 18(8), pp.851-860.

Yanuck SF, Pizzorno J, Messier H, Fitzgerald KN., 2020. Evidence Supporting a Phased Immuno-physiological Approach to COVID-19 From Prevention Through Recovery, *Integrative Medicine,Vol. 19, No. S1, Epub Ahead of Print*

Larrieu, T. and Layé, S., 2018. Food for Mood: Relevance of Nutritional Omega-3 Fatty Acids for Depression and Anxiety. *Frontiers in Physiology*, 9.

Calder, P., Carr, A., Gombart, A. and Eggersdorfer, M., 2020. Optimal Nutritional Status for a Well-Functioning Immune System Is an Important Factor to Protect against Viral Infections. *Nutrients*, 12(4), p.1181.

Rondanelli, M., Miccono, A., Lamburghini, S., Avanzato, I., Riva, A., Allegrini, P., Faliva, M., Peroni, G., Nichetti, M. and Perna, S., 2018. Self-Care for Common Colds: The Pivotal Role of Vitamin D, Vitamin C, Zinc, and Echinacea in Three Main Immune Interactive Clusters (Physical Barriers, Innate and Adaptive Immunity) Involved during an Episode of Common Colds— Practical Advice on Dosages and on the Time to Take These Nutrients/Botanicals in order to Prevent or Treat Common Colds. *Evidence-Based Complementary and Alternative Medicine*, 2018, pp.1-36.

Ullah, H., Akhtar, M., Hussain, F. and Imran, M., 2016. Effects of Sugar, Salt and Distilled Water on White BloodCells and Platelet Cells. *Journal of Tumor*, 4(1), pp.354-358.

Martineau, A., Jolliffe, D., Hooper, R., Greenberg, L., Aloia, J., Bergman, P., Dubnov-Raz, G., Esposito, S., Ganmaa, D., Goodall, E., Grant, C., Janssens, W., Laaksi, I., Manaseki-Holland, S., Murdoch, D., Neale, R., Rees, J., Simpson, S., Stelmach, I., Kumar, G., Urashima, M. and Camargo, C., 2016. S102 Vitamin d supplementation to prevent acute respiratory infections: systematic review and meta-analysis of individual participant data. *Thorax*, 71(Suppl 3), pp.A60.2-A61.

Hulisz, D., 2004. Efficacy of Zinc Against Common Cold Viruses: An Overview. *Journal of the American Pharmacists Association*, 44(5), pp.594-603.

Maares, M. and Haase, H., 2016. Zinc and immunity: An essential interrelation. *Archives of Biochemistry and Biophysics*, 611, pp.58-65.

Kinker, B., 2014. Quercetin: A Promising Treatment for the Common Cold. *Journal of Ancient Diseases & Preventive Remedies*, 02(02).

Morris, D., Khurasany, M., Nguyen, T., Kim, J., Guilford, F., Mehta, R., Gray, D., Saviola, B. and Venketaraman, V., 2013. Glutathione and infection. *Biochimica et Biophysica Acta (BBA) - General Subjects*, 1830(5), pp.3329-3349.

Meydani, S., Leka, L., Fine, B., Dallal, G., Keusch, G., Singh, M. and Hamer, D., 2004. Vitamin E and Respiratory Tract Infections in Elderly Nursing Home Residents. *JAMA*, 292(7), p.828.

Kunnumakkara, A., Bordoloi, D., Padmavathi, G., Monisha, J., Roy, N., Prasad, S. and Aggarwal, B., 2016. Curcumin, the golden nutraceutical: multitargeting for multiple chronic diseases. *British Journal of Pharmacology*, 174(11), pp.1325-1348.

Müller, S., März, R., Schmolz, M., Drewelow, B., Eschmann, K. and Meiser, P., 2012. Placebo-controlled Randomized Clinical Trial on the Immunomodulating Activities of Low- and High-Dose Bromelain after Oral Administration - New Evidence on the Antiinflammatory Mode of Action of Bromelain. *Phytotherapy Research*, 27(2), pp.199-204.

Dai, X., Stanilka, J., Rowe, C., Esteves, E., Nieves, C., Spaiser, S., Christman, M., Langkamp-Henken, B. and Percival, S., 2015. ConsumingLentinula edodes(Shiitake) Mushrooms Daily Improves Human Immunity: A Randomized Dietary Intervention in Healthy Young Adults. *Journal of the American College of Nutrition*, 34(6), pp.478-487.

Matsumoto, K., Yamada, H., Takuma, N., Niino, H. and Sagesaka, Y., 2011. Effects of Green Tea Catechins and Theanine on Preventing Influenza Infection among Healthcare Workers: A Randomized Controlled Trial. *BMC Complementary and Alternative Medicine*, 11(1).

Lin, S., Ho, C., Chuo, W., Li, S., Wang, T. and Lin, C., 2017. Effective inhibition of MERS-CoV infection by resveratrol. *BMC Infectious Diseases*, 17(1).

Irwin, M., 2019. Sleep and inflammation: partners in sickness and in health. *Nature Reviews Immunology*, 19(11), pp.702-715.

Ibarra-Coronado, E., Pantaleón-Martínez, A., Velazquéz-Moctezuma, J., Prospéro-García, O., Méndez-Díaz, M., Pérez-Tapia, M., Pavón, L. and Morales-Montor, J., 2015. The Bidirectional Relationship between Sleep and Immunity against Infections. *Journal of Immunology Research*, 2015, pp.1-14.

Shi, L., Chen, S., Ma, M., Bao, Y., Han, Y., Wang, Y., Shi, J., Vitiello, M. and Lu, L., 2018. Sleep disturbances increase the risk of dementia: A systematic review and meta-analysis. *Sleep Medicine Reviews*, 40, pp.4-16.

Favero, G., Franceschetti, L., Bonomini, F., Rodella, L. and Rezzani, R., 2017. Melatonin as an Anti-Inflammatory Agent Modulating Inflammasome Activation. *International Journal of Endocrinology*, 2017, pp.1-13.

Ricker, M. and Haas, W., 2017. Anti-Inflammatory Diet in Clinical Practice: A Review. *Nutrition in Clinical Practice*, 32(3), pp.318-325.

The Power of Human Connection and Open Communication
by Sadie Restorick

There is no denying it, we live in a fast-paced world. Despite the growing emergence of experts encouraging us all to be more mindful and regularly put our foot on the proverbial psychological brake, it would seem that our modern-day demanding schedules and hectic lifestyles make it seemingly difficult to be in the moment. We hurtle from place to place, juggling multiple demands and can often find ourselves mentally detached from the present moment, our nomadic minds drifting off in one direction before getting dragged the opposite way again. Not only is this detrimental to our mental health and wellbeing, but it is also highly impactful on the quality of our relationships and our connections with others. It is common to find ourselves engaging in conversation but being easily distracted, rushing interactions because we are so preoccupied with everything that we need to get done. In essence, our capacity to actively connect with another person is hindered due to our haste to speed up the exchange because there are other things on our to-do list.

Sound familiar at all?

It is an easy trap to fall into. I can recall times when I personally have rushed a conversation because I had other things whirling around in my mind. People talk to me in training workshops about times that they would be only partially listening to their family because they were thinking about their work. My friends and I can go months without seeing each other because, quite simply, we are too busy. Yet the irony is that the busier we are, and the more stressed and overwhelmed we feel, the more we need to invest the time in those real and genuine interactions with others.

In spring 2020, the reality of just how important these connections are became utterly apparent. The lockdown status and enforced social distancing meant that something that so many took for granted, such as the ability to embrace loved ones, was deeply craved. As stress levels heightened, collectively we were reminded that at our core we are social creatures. Mental health concerns and the impact of loneliness were experienced on a widespread scale as many became isolated away from the people they love. Rippling through our communities, there became a heightened, conscious recognition of the absolute need to be with other people, particularly during times of adversity.

There are lessons we can all take from this time about the significance of our interactions with others, the depth of our connections and the ways in which we communicate. In this chapter, I will be exploring the science behind human connection and how we can all optimise the quality of our connections with others, particularly during times of stress and adversity, and how this can have a profound impact on our wellbeing. I will explore simple ways you can reflect on the way you communicate to build more authentic and open relationships with others, and why this is so important for a healthy and positive way of life.

The Science of Social Connection

It is an instinctive and primeval response to yearn to be around others during times of stress. Forming a huddle, keeping each other safe from threats and generating a mutual, soothing reassurance is pretty much hardwired into us to maximise our chances of survival.

This is demonstrated by our biological response to social connections. When we experience love (either romantic or platonic), attraction and connection, our body is quickly flooded with a cocktail of chemicals which include dopamine, testosterone, estrogen, vasopressin and oxytocin (which triggers the release of serotonin). This response is directed by a neural network called the vagus nerve which wanders (vagus is Latin for 'wandering') throughout the entire body, transmitting messages millions of times a day and affecting multiple systems in the body.

Think of this vagus nerve as the connecting cable between your emotions and your body. It is plugged into how you feel and feeds this to different parts of your body. Have you ever felt that crippling chest pain from grief, loss, hurt or rejection that people refer to as a broken heart? What about when you feel apprehension, dread or suspicion about a person or situation, and talk about having a gut instinct that something is going to go wrong? Emotions are strongly experienced throughout the body due to this connecting cable and as such, we can strengthen our bodies and our health through the positive emotional response generated by our sense of connection.

This connecting cable is also the primary force behind the parasympathetic nervous system which regulates your 'rest-and-digest' or 'tend-and-befriend' response. This is the opposite of the more commonly known 'fight or flight' response, which is driven by the sympathetic nervous system and triggered when we are faced with a physical or psychological threat. Research behind the 'tend-and-befriend' response indicates that in the face of stress, people often respond by tending to and affiliating with others. This drive is often compared to the way that the body alerts us to other needs, such as hunger, and that our brains signal out a message in the face of stress by releasing oxytocin, which urges us to seek out other people (Taylor & Master, 2011). Now some of you may recall that this is a hormone that we have already mentioned when we referred to the cocktail of happy hormones. This is because oxytocin actually has a dual function; it provides us with a physiological reward when we maintain social contact during times of low stress, yet when we experience heightened stress, it is also released to compel us to seek out others.

The points outlined above allude to some of the many reasons that the enforced temporary 'antidote' to prevent the contraction of the virus during the 2020 pandemic was found to be so alarming to many. It meant that our basic need to gather in the face of danger was made impossible, leading to a different kind of emerging risk as a result of this temporary cure: loneliness. Loneliness is more substantially dangerous to our psychological and physical wellbeing than many realise, with studies claiming the health risks of loneliness to be at a similar level to that of smoking (Holt-Lunstad, Smith & Layton, 2010). Evidently, it is apparent that we all need to seek out ways to optimise our opportunities for human interaction, both now and in the future.

As such, the remainder of this chapter will seek to explore some practical ways to enrich your life with the support of others.

Develop and Optimise Your Support Network

Not all social interactions are created equal. As such, sufficient support networks and human connections to meet and exceed your basic needs are not simply a matter of quantity and playing a numbers game. Consideration must be given to the type and depth of the social contact and support needed and provided. Think of your network of social support as a spectrum, with complete isolation at one end and deep, emotional and practical support at the other. Also bear in mind that truly authentic and valuable connections are reciprocal, so to generate and sustain these connections both parties need to invest in the connection and mutually support each other.

Essentially, from a social perspective, all you truly need to thrive is a handful of people who provide you with sufficient, supportive contact, particularly in the face of stress, anxiety or fear. Such a level of comfort and reassurance has proven to help individuals feel more empowered to face fears and overcome uncertainty. In fact, this is a method to treat phobias using exposure therapy, whereby an individual is gradually exposed to the subject of the fear, with the support of the therapist being used to help the person to explore their fear far more than they could do alone. However, if we are going to look into developing a robust support network to meet your diverse and varied needs, it is important to undertake an audit of your current network and what areas might need development.

Take a moment to think about your current support network. Naturally, there are inevitably different types of support so each type needs due consideration. Commonly these include:

- Emotional support: This is most typically associated with support networks and relates to those around you who provide you with emotional support. They are typically high in emotional intelligence. For example, if you experience a very traumatic time, a close friend might call every day for the first few weeks afterwards just to see how you are doing and to let you know that they care.

- Practical help: These are the people who are good with practical tips, advice and guidance. They tend to be composed, good problem solvers and very logical. For example, if you are looking to talk to someone about a problem with your career, they might help you put together a plan of action and provide advice on what steps to take.
- Perspective sharing: These are people who may face similar challenges and who are able to share their perspective, experiences and knowledge with you to help you gain a different insight or think of a different way to handle them. For example, if you are struggling with childcare issues, they may share ideas on how they dealt with similar situations in their family.
- Sharing information: These are people who are knowledgeable in a certain area and provide facts about a specific situation. They are resourceful and generally quite helpful, giving you the time and information needed. For example, a friend who recently has been made redundant might help with advice on the next steps to take.

Think about these different types of support and who you have in each different area, making sure to consider various situations that you have faced in the past and what/who helped.

It might help to consider the following questions to start to establish this network:

- Who are the people in your life you can turn to when you need to talk to someone?
- Who is your go-to person you can call when something really great happens and you want to share the news? This is often someone with whom you have a deep connection.
- Who helps when regular, everyday tasks seem overwhelming? You may want to break this down to different areas in your life such as work and home.
- Who faces similar challenges to you? Think about people in your network who might share the same obstacles in their life.
- What people in your communities might have faced similar challenges to you?

Develop a list of people for each type of support based on your current needs and challenges, and use this as a go-to resource to edit and grow over time. Try to avoid limiting your scope to present contacts; take the time to consider old connections that might need rebuilding, as well as potential new ones that could be worth nurturing. Remember, though: the key is to build mutual connections and bonds.

Show Compassion and Create Micro-Moments of Connection

Whilst taking the steps to develop a support network and build meaningful connections with those close to you, there are other, quite intrinsically powerful ways to develop your range of social connections. Barbara Fredrickson (2013), a leading researcher on emotions and relationships, emphasises the importance of small, positive interactions and micro-moments of connection. Fredrickson uses the term 'positivity resonance' to emphasise that a shared positive experience or emotion, even if fleeting and with a stranger, is a critical investment in the wellbeing of both parties (2013). The increased sense of connectedness from these moments also generates an increase in vagal tone, the level of activity generated by the previously mentioned vagus nerve. When we consider that the higher the level of a person's vagal tone, the quicker their body is able to relax from stress, we can start to really understand how mighty these micro-moments can be.

I am sure that you have all experienced these moments. A momentary interaction with a stranger about the weather, a friendly chat with the supermarket checkout operator or a smile at the person who holds the door open for you? Perhaps a compliment for the person ahead of you in the queue? On my daily dog walks I regularly chat with fellow dog walkers and admire their furry companions; it might appear trivial but the cumulative effect of these moments are highly impactful. They literally boost our connectivity with our community and spread a contagious message of positivity that has a ripple effect from person to person.

The impact of this message is particularly strong when we show warmth and compassion, as this strengthens the quality of the connection. In fact, quite ironically, showing kindness to others and giving back in some form has a significantly more positive impact on us than the recipient. Science actually shows that our cells are able to discriminate between self-gratification (or hedonistic wellbeing) and self-transcendent actions which contribute to a greater good or have a sense of meaning (or eudemonic wellbeing), with the latter strengthening our immune system (Fredrickson et al, 2015).

Every day, each one of us can maximise upon the power of these brief moments. So how can you create more micro-moments built on compassion and kindness?

- Embrace any opportunity to actively connect with people that you see. Even if from a distance, a smile, a compliment or a simple nod of acknowledgement can make a big difference. Start small if you feel apprehensive about engaging in a conversation.

- Learn about compassionate meditation, a practice which helps to open the heart and increase levels of interconnectivity. In quiet moments, think of loving and kind phrases and direct them towards a particular person in a way that is intentional, such as: May you be safe. May you be well (Fredrickson, 2013).

- Think about how you can insert random acts of kindness into your day-to-day life. Doing something thoughtful for another person without any expectation for anything in return can be incredibly simple but effective.

- Check in on other people and see how they are. Ensure that this includes work colleagues as well as friends and family. Show genuine concern for others and actively identify signs of concern, making time to ensure that others know you care. The gift of your time is more valuable than you may realise.

Build and Nurture Your Communities

Relational cultures fall into three categories: cultures of control, cultures of indifference and cultures of connection (Stallard,

2015). With a culture of control, those with power and status rule over other people. Cultures of indifference are highly common in the present day, and this relates to the points made earlier in the chapter about our pace of life and lack of time to invest in healthy interactions with others. What we all need to move towards is the third cultural category, cultures of connection. Within these types of collectives, people are caring towards others and reach out to those in need, enabling each person to feel an immensely powerful and reassuring sense of belonging.

When we apply this way of thinking to the way we collectively respond in the face of a crisis, we can see that by coming together and being united in facing the challenges as one, it is possible to build and nurture empathic connections based on a shared understanding of what has been faced together. This helps to cultivate a culture of shared experience and unity, essentially contributing to a culture of connection, as opposed to a culture of control or a culture of indifference. Consider how you can take conscious steps to create cultures of connection within your different communities to enhance a collective and mutual sense of social support. Think about the following questions:

- A community provides a sense of security and stability and is usually driven by a shared purpose, goal or interest. Do you have a community for each 'hat that you wear?' For example, if you are a working parent, could you join an online network or group of other working parents? If you are a keen runner, are you part of a running group? How connected are you with your local neighbourhood community?
- Think about the communities you belong to, large and small. This may include your local neighbourhood community,

online communities, your workplace communities or hobbies relating to your interests. How often do you connect with those in that community and how engaged are you? What is the quality of those connections?

- What steps can you take to contribute to a collective sense of wellbeing in your different respective communities and spread positive emotions to others by giving back? How can you creatively and proactively help others within that community based on an empathic understanding of what they might need?

- When thinking about your online communities, consider the way in which you interact with posts and content. Simply browsing and intermittently liking posts is one-sided and can lead to heightened feelings of loneliness and wasted emotional effort. Actively responding and engaging by commenting and creating new posts more readily enhances levels of connectedness.

Authentic and Open Communication

One thing that cannot be ignored is the effectiveness of your communication when connecting with others. The quality of our interactions and our conversations, virtual or otherwise, relies on our ability to actively consider the way in which we communicate. This is a two-way street so firstly, let's look at one of the biggest roadblocks that people encounter: their ability to listen.

Knowing how to actively listen is a skill. It takes patience, self-awareness and a genuine desire to understand. It is all too common for people to believe they are competent listeners; after all, we engage in conversations every day. But unfortunately, we are often not fully present in these face-to-face interactions - we are only partly engaged, with our minds wandering in all sorts of different directions. In fact, the average person speaks at a rate of about 125 words per minute, yet our brains have the mental capacity to process 400 words per minute.

This means we get distracted; we fail to interpret meaning accurately and we miss vital clues. The truth is, in this fast-paced, overloaded and high-pressure world, most people are pretty poor at listening. The sad result is that people stop talking, a fact which is considerably detrimental when we are trying to create meaningful connections.

When you ask someone "How are you?", how often do you truly listen to the answer? When you are chatting with a friend on FaceTime, do you pay attention to their body language, their tone of voice, the message behind their words?

When engaging in a conversation with a friend or colleague, particularly when discussing subjects that are emotive or personal, the key is really to create a dynamic where both parties feel that they are in a shared, psychologically safe space where they can express themselves in an honest way. Work to create an environment where the other person feels able to speak up and truly be heard. A good way to encourage this is to lead by example. There is a great power that comes from expressing vulnerability and having the courage to speak from the heart. It demonstrates that you trust the other person and that your connection is one of mutual respect and empathy. Furthermore, it enables you to share how you are feeling, particularly during times of stress, and move away from any natural tendencies to suppress or ignore certain emotions. As Brene Brown (2010) states, "Vulnerability is the birthplace of connection and the path to the feeling of worthiness. If it doesn't feel vulnerable, the sharing is probably not constructive."

Doing these things and communicating in an intentional and effective way comes more naturally to some than others. Your level of emotional intelligence will impact how comfortably you adopt this approach, but there are things everyone can do to build this muscle.

So, what things can you start to consider?

- When communicating virtually, do your best to simulate in-person communication using video calls to provide the natural non-verbal cues that form part of our usual conversations. These signals help to enhance the quality of our message, increase engagement and prevent miscommunication.

- Work on actively listening by removing any distractions and being fully present in your interactions, virtual or otherwise. Demonstrate your understanding by summarising and use prompts, both verbal and non-verbal, to encourage disclosure. Always remember that the focus is on the person talking and understanding their perspective.

- If you are struggling and want to reach out, remember the importance of being truthful and authentic, and of shedding the lines of defence and fears of judgement. Openly express what you feel and what you need in that moment.

Summary

We have ascertained that our need to socially connect is as fundamental as our need for food and water and without it, our psychological wellbeing starts to diminish and suffer. Whilst times of crisis can threaten our ability to connect in the ways to which we have become accustomed, with every challenge and trauma comes an opportunity for growth and learning. In the face of the 2020 pandemic, we fought together against a common enemy and united as a global community in the face of extreme trauma and distress. These times can equip us all with insight and knowledge of what can be achieved when we join forces with each other, show courage in the face of adversity and build genuine social connections with others. Every single one of us has faced the reality of a life of isolation, with loved ones kept at a distance. Therefore, from this moment on, we can all cultivate a genuinely profound and heartfelt appreciation for the power of human connection and social contact.

If you would like any more information or access to any of our free training courses on managing your wellbeing, please contact me at hello@weworkwell.co.uk

Connect with me on Linkedin: https://www.linkedin.com/in/ sadiehopson/

Visit www.weworkwell.co.uk

About the Author

Sadie Restorick is a speaker, consultant, trainer and published academic scholar specialising in workplace mental health and wellbeing and psychosocial risk management. She is a BA Communications graduate and has extensively studied training needs analysis and design and theories of communication within groups and organisations. She holds a diploma in Mental Health Awareness and a diploma with Distinction from the Fellowship of Associated Stress Consultants. She has been awarded an MSc with Distinction in Workplace Health and Wellbeing from the globally recognised University of Nottingham. Specific areas of study include the phenomenon of presenteeism, the effectiveness of interventions for tackling stress in the workplace, the impact of digital overload and burnout and the emerging risk of increased physical inactivity across the working population.

Sadie is the Founder and Managing Director of two businesses, Euthenia Touch and We Work Well. She has written for a number of trade journals and publications including Personnel Today, Safety and Health Practitioner (SHP), Occupational Health, Training Journal, Business Leader, Ergonoma Journal and Stress News. She has appeared on national BBC One television, BBC Radio and Talk Radio, providing expert advice on subjects relating to her field. Sadie is also a national champion for the 'Time to Change' mental health campaign and has worked extensively to support individuals with mental health problems and end mental health discrimination in the community. Voluntary work includes the development of campaigns and seminars at local colleges to help support youth mental health and recognise the challenges faced by the younger generation.

Sadie has worked in the field for over 10 years providing consultancy and training to some of the largest companies in the world. She has worked with companies of all sizes to develop mental health strategies that are fit for purpose, auditing organisations on their existing strategies and helping stakeholders develop an approach that fits the needs of their people and their businesses.

A passionate mental health advocate, in her spare time Sadie regularly competes in events to raise money for mental health charities, recently completing a half marathon and the London to Brighton bike ride.

References

Brown, B., 2010. The Power of Vulnerability. Retrieved from ttps://www.ted.com/talks/brene_brown_the_power_of_vulnerability

Fredrickson, B., 2013. *Love 2.0: How our supreme emotion affects everything we feel, think, do, and become*. Avery.

Fredrickson, B.L., Grewen, K.M., Algoe, S.B., Firestine, A.M., Arevalo, J.M., Ma, J. and Cole, S.W., 2015. Psychological well-being and the human conserved transcriptional response to adversity. *PloS one*, *10*(3).

Holt-Lunstad, J., Smith, T.B. and Layton, J.B., 2010. Social relationships and mortality risk: a meta-analytic review. *PLoS med*, *7*(7), p.e1000316.

Stallard, M.L., 2015. *Connection culture: The competitive advantage of shared identity, empathy, and understanding at work*. American Society for Training and Development.

Taylor, S.E. and Master, S.L., 2011. Social responses to stress: The tend-and-befriend model. *The handbook of stress science: Biology, psychology, and health*, pp.101-109.

Trauma and Us
by Lucy Batham-Read

Introduction

Trauma is never the event but our memory of it and how it made us feel. Inevitably, what you define as trauma and what I define as trauma may be different; it is certainly not for either of us to judge each other's lives and how we cope. What we can agree upon is that trauma is the experience of not being seen or heard and disconnecting from ourselves. If too much is thrown at someone, they will begin to seek more of what is familiar and fear anything else.

What must be remembered is that fear is part of being human and our goal is to allow the fear, yet trust that little bit more - not necessarily become fearless. Fear and trust cannot exist in our minds at the same time and when we notice which place we are operating from, we also give ourselves the time to shift our perception. Sometimes this is all it takes to go from impossible to "I'm Possible." Remember: regardless of how much fear is surrounding you, take heed that fear only sells until we stop buying into it and when we do stop buying into it, trust and synchronicity become awesome partners in crime. The current pandemic is 'trauma' but like all trauma it can lead us to an awakening where we can reclaim ourselves and our sense of purpose.

The traumas we face make us who we are and sometimes they are simply gifts in ugly packaging. We have to learn to acknowledge how life makes us feel whilst using the past to guide us, not control us, and equally learn to be kind enough to ourselves to accept we are all doing the best we can with what we know now. When we know better, we will choose to do better and with this we learn to live with less regret, shame, fear and resentment which in turn reduces our risk of 'dis-ease' of the mind, body and spirit. Furthermore, when we learn true wellbeing is not the absence of 'dis-ease' but the mind, body, spirit connection, we start to notice each sliding door and accept what we are facing, whilst equally having a perception of the present moment that represents both our reality and our body chemistry.

> **"Life is change. Growth is optional. Choose wisely."**
>
> **Karen Kaiser Clark**

Transformation and living well is not always a switch. More often it represents a gauge and with it, the ability to ride the waves, weather the storms and trust life that little bit more than you fear it. The beauty is that you don't have to flip a button and learn it all at once. We are all always a work in progress and life is our greatest teacher.

I have learnt that change is constant but growth optional, and it usually requires us to be willing to unlearn what we think we know in order to learn what we need to know now. Trauma will happen to us all in various forms but when we have a growth mindset, we reduce the risk of holding onto belief systems that are not serving us well and we learn how to let go of ones that are not ours to own. It does not make us invincible but it does make us resilient. Lessons are all around us. Failure can become our greatest teacher. Mistakes can become our greatest mentors. You are the author. You hold the pen. You get to learn and read and write your own masterpiece, chapter by chapter, line by line, letter by letter. Write well but be willing to edit often and never be afraid to shout "plot twist," nor be so strong you refuse to find courage through vulnerability. You are the hero of your own story, but self-ownership and resilience are key to a life well lived.

Throughout this process, it is important to remember that 'keep calm and carry on' is not always good for your wellbeing. You cannot be selfless unless you are equally willing to be selfish. I used to really resent the word 'grateful' because I had been taught to 'put others before thyself' and that there was always someone worse off than me. That mindset allowed me to put myself so far down the list of priorities that my body screamed, and it was only when I learnt to look after myself first that I was able to help others from a full cup, and truly live with a grateful heart and an open mind. We cannot expect life to work for us if we continually seek distraction from ourselves, but once we get the right connection internally our external world will reflect this too - both by the situations we find ourselves in and the people we are surrounded by. Notice everything and be brave enough to adjust your sails when you need to.

Take the time to get clear about where you are going and what you'd like to accomplish. Write this down. Then focus. Whatever we focus on grows. Get clear and then laser focus on your most meaningful priorities. Don't sweat the other stuff. Keep it simple and focus on what you care most about.

So what are some of the things we need to remember if we are to stay well in mind and body, no matter what?

Your starting point involves being honest with yourself and taking responsibility for all your past choices. No matter where you are on your health and wellbeing journey, you cannot make progress if you're still beating yourself up for laziness or poor choices in the past, be they emotions, food, exercise and/or choices in life. You have to accept your past choices, come into the present moment and start exactly where you are. The exciting part is that you have the power to make a new choice in every moment and move beyond past limitations and perceived failures.

For now, we will approach your ability to thrive no matter what happens by approaching it all pragmatically.

We will follow these steps to understand and evaluate:

1. Forgiveness
2. Acceptance
3. Feelings
4. Wellbeing
5. Values
6. Clarity
7. Intentions

HOW DO WE DO THIS?

FORGIVENESS

The leaping point for everything begins with forgiveness. You cannot successfully move forward in life and create a healthy mind and body if you're living with guilt, resentment or regret. It could be a person, an event, a failed business, a lost dream or a broken relationship. Regardless of who and/or what it is, the journey begins with self-forgiveness for our own part in not knowing then what we know now.

Anything you invest your energy in uses up your precious life force. A good way to begin to do this is to write yourself or someone else a letter that you never post. Forgiveness happens inside of you so no one ever need know about the letter, and the most important thing is to stop holding the pain in your mind and body.

It does not mean we condone others for their part, but it does mean we do not remain prisoner of the past and that we forgive ourselves enough to let go of whatever it is that happened. We can remember what it taught us without storing it in our mind and body like a ticking time bomb, or worse still - pass it onto another generation for them to bury yet further within their DNA.

ACCEPTANCE

Nothing is a failure unless we repeat a pattern that we are conscious does not serve us well. Self-acceptance is possibly the longest journey we ever make but if we connect the right dots, we live with less regret and much more peace of mind and wellness of body. Acceptance of what is enables us to instantly become open to what will be.

Steps to Acceptance:

- Observe the reality of your situation
- Pay attention to the bodily signs of fighting that reality
- Acknowledge that you are reacting to something you cannot change

- Remind yourself what the reality is, even if it is upsetting
- Acknowledge that some sort of history led up to this moment and don't judge
- Accept this reality with your whole being: your mind, body and spirit

(Do this over again and again until you have reached acceptance.)

FEELINGS

Learning to know the truth by the way it feels to us is vital if we are to pivot when life throws us a curveball, and if we are going to constantly make choices that take us closer to where we are heading, not further away. Our intuition is the one thing that is working exclusively for us; learning to trust it requires us to feel everything - the good and the bad - without seeking distraction or validation outside of ourselves to be OK with how we feel.

Fear is simply a guide but we must learn to allow it through us and not into us. We must also learn to trust the truth by the way it feels to us but allow ourselves to feel without judgement, something that is not easy when we think the answers to life lie in control. If this is us when we lose control, we find we had anxiety all along.

We don't need all the answers in life; we simply need to understand that by doing our part without looking over our shoulder our feelings will start to 'ground' us and we begin to allow more, control less, trust more, fear less.

WELLBEING

Your health is your pension and a reflection of your choices and your lifestyle. Much of our health and wellbeing begins with our emotions and how we process them, and feelings that are left misunderstood have a habit of manifesting into physical conditions. When we understand our current health and how to listen to our own sat-nav and what is right for our bodies, we learn how to make good choices. It all begins with a regulated nervous system and a strong gut-brain connection. Not only does your future health depend on your commitment to this, but so does your children's. True wellbeing is not the absence of 'dis-ease' but the mind, body, spirit connection. Some of this is diet and exercise, but not all of it.

VALUES AND BELIEF SYSTEMS

Values and belief systems are your compass point to what really matters to you. Do you even know what yours are, and are they yours or ones that were passed onto you? Too many people have never had the opportunity to define their own values; they just adopted those of others and as time evolved, have become dutybound to values that do not perhaps resonate with their own heart and soul, leading to confusion as to the truth of themselves and often, resentment of their lives.

Your belief system and values in life are the underlying motivation for your choices. Identifying your core values is an important step in reaching your goals. When your head and heart are aligned, you will easily achieve your goals because you'll do the work. They should of course be reviewed regularly because just like us, life changes and we need to constantly adapt and pivot.

Start with our list and come up with your top 5. You might be surprised.

Adventure	Fulfilment	Kindness	Self-reliance	Balance	Forgiveness
Knowledge	Service	Confidence	Fun	Love	Spirituality
Control	God	Lifestyle	Strength	Creativity	Growth
Marriage	Success	Discipline	Happiness	Peace of Mind	Truth
Education	Health	Power	Unity	Faith	Self-expression
Progress	Wealth	Family	Honesty	Reason	Financial Security
Security	Humour	Respect	Friends	Integrity	Independence
Freedom	Wisdom	Hope			

CLARITY

When it is clear you need change, you need to reset clear intentions and see in your mind's eye what you want to create for yourself and your life. Dive into the big 'why' behind wanting these things.

Clarity comes when our dreams are broken down into bite-size chunks. They give our life meaning, a sense of purpose and a feeling of fulfilment. Clarity helps us know why we want something. If we cannot come up with a strong enough why or purpose for wanting our goal, then we won't have the motivation to overcome all the challenges and obstacles that we will, without doubt, meet along the way. Our why comes from our core values and what is most important to us. If our goals are not congruent with our core values, we will constantly sabotage ourselves – or we may achieve our goal but will not be able to sustain it. Or, equally as damaging, we will invent constant glass ceilings that become all-encompassing and we'll miss out on the joy of life because, as we know, everything can and sometimes does change in an instant. I was once told never to discuss my dreams with anyone until I was totally in a place where I fully believed they would happen because once I was, my spirit would threaten others' fears and that fear would be reflected back to me if I was not strong enough to stand tall.

Questions to ask yourself:

- What do I want?
- Why do I want it?
- How will I make it happen?
- What are the actions I need to take?
- When will I have it?
- Who do I need to help me to achieve my goal?
- Which fears and limiting beliefs do I need to let go of to reach this goal?

INTENTIONS

When change knocks on our door it makes us question everything, but when our intentions are clear and we have a why, our purpose becomes clear too. Our purpose is the fuel that fires our inner motivation and becomes the driving force behind all our choices, actions and behaviours.

Maybe some of these questions will help you understand your purpose now. Remember, it does not need to be something big; it could be just to create a happy home with fun and laughter where everyone feels safe, heard and valued. You don't have to have all the answers - just one of them might spark the question you need to delve into right now.

- Who am I and why am I here?
- What legacy do I want to leave?
- What gifts and talents do I wish to share with the world?
- What have I learnt in my life that I can pass onto others?
- What is my message?
- What makes me come alive?
- What does life want from me?
- What is it that wants to be expressed through me?

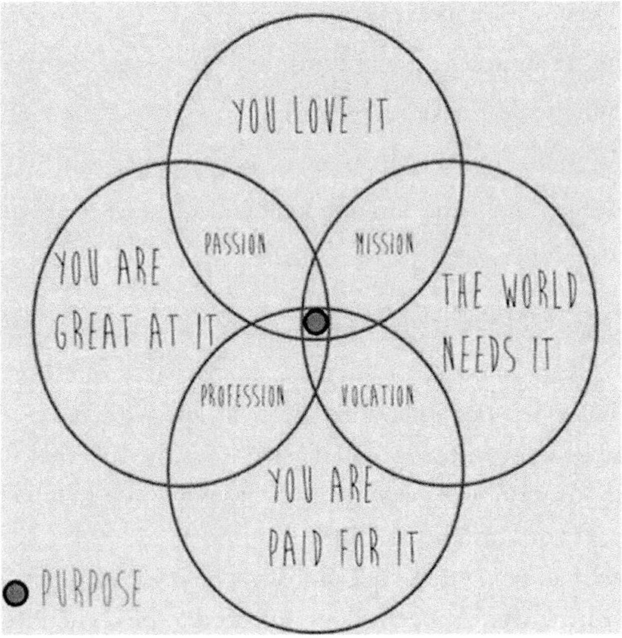
YOU LOVE IT
YOU ARE GREAT AT IT
THE WORLD NEEDS IT
YOU ARE PAID FOR IT
PASSION
MISSION
PROFESSION
VOCATION
PURPOSE

FINDING HAPPINESS

Everyone thinks they just want to be happy, but it is a choice, not a destination, and it does not come from anything outside of us. To be truly happy in life we need to be content in the present moment, and to do this we must be honest with ourselves and not just accept what is, but trust what will be. This reality can be truly uncomfortable but to live a life in colour, not just black and white, we must equally be willing to fail. It is in this gap that we find the peace of mind and wellness of body to live our lives well and know that when we get to the end of the line, we have lived with few regrets and a generation behind us that is stronger than the one before.

One of the most powerful pieces of advice when it comes to the process of living your life well is to get out of your head and into your heart. There needs to be a shift from the buzzing mental vibration that blocks the energy, to a state of flow and surrender that creates the space to allow your desires to manifest into your reality in a simple, natural and effortless way. This happens when your nervous system is regulated and your gut-brain connection strong, and you get on with being the best version of yourself each day whilst keeping your eye very firmly on your why and allowing the how.

It's not easy to put a lifetime of learning into a few short pages but I trust this will have given you an insight into how you can take your power back if life has thrown you a curveball, or if you are still operating under the paradigm that trauma is the event as opposed to the effect. Our ability to see life as being full of opportunity, not obstacles, always depends on our perception at the time and our ability to choose connection, and not seek distraction from the truth, is dependent on how well we are connected with our own truth. Yet first and foremost, we must learn to be the perfectly imperfect humans we all are and not be fearless but fear less, and trust more.

About the Author

I am a qualified wellbeing life coach with diplomas in Mindfulness and CBT. My interest is the nervous system and our own unique gut-brain connection. I also use Edutherapy with my work. I am also an Ambassador at St Peter and St James Hospice to help with raising awareness of the hospice's work, not only for end of life care but also for those living with cancer. As well as my private work I also work within the NHS, working with children and young people with serious mental health problems and eating disorders. I am constantly learning and seeing how functional medicine can help us all live well for longer, no matter what our starting point.

My curiosity into wellbeing started with my daughter and her constant problems with her nose and throat, and the potential threat of her having an operation to remove her tonsils and her adenoids at the age of 2. She had been using nebulisers and inhalers as well as having constant steroids since she was 6 months old, and having been given a date for surgery, in desperation we turned to homeopathy in the hope we could help her both sleep through the night and allow her to breathe properly without resorting to surgery.

That was now over 19 years ago and not only did she not have the operation, but she has not used inhalers or nebulisers for years. She does, however, have a resistance to traditional medicine and 'needles!'

In truth, however, my daughter's 'dis-ease' was in fact my opportunity to find out who I really was and it was the unravelling of me that was really needed in order to help her. Until I came across Functional Medicine, I too had 'suffered' a catalogue of physical symptoms pretty much since birth, including asthma, eczema, IBS, glandular fever, chronic fatigue and arthritis. I had also attempted an overdose at 22 when I found myself jobless, living in a bedsit, broke and frightened, was tested for cancer, suffered severe postnatal depression and had a termination for medical reasons at 18 weeks.

Until then, I had assumed my 'conditions' were just bad luck and would never have guessed there was a common thread to it all. Even the overdose had been 'pigeon-holed' into a blip and one I had never truly discussed with anyone. After all, they had certainly not stopped me from working around the world, running an IT company and living the 'high life' of the 80s and 90s and to the outside world, I had it all and was just 'lucky.' Clearly, however, it turned out I had an awful lot of onion layers that needed unravelling in order to find the truth of me and in turn, fully connect with my own mind, body and soul. It was only then that I was in a position to find my own wellbeing balance so I could then really start to live an 'abundant' life, whatever that meant to me.

What I discovered was that all of my 'dis-ease' stemmed from deep seated 'trauma' and PTSD, which at the root of it all was a very weak immune system, under which was a completely de-regulated central nervous system - none of which I had any idea existed, and all of which had begun right from even before my entry into this world. All of it was 'fixable' through functional medicine and my own alignment with me.

From my own experiences I have learnt so much about epigenetics, the central nervous system, the vagus nerve and how, when it comes to our wellbeing, everything is about the cell to soul connection and our perception of the world around us.

Unravelling our onion layers can indeed be painful, but they also set us free. Learning to align with ourselves not only means we are healthy in mind, body and soul but it also enables us to live the life we love, if we are bold enough to imagine and brave enough to claim it. We will, however, always require a helping hand every now and then.

These days you will find me living in a beautiful farmhouse in the Sussex countryside with my husband of 25 years, 3 children aged 21, 19 and 15, a dog called Wellington and a cat named Boo. I am incredibly grateful to now be healthy in mind, body and soul, but it is never something I take for granted and I am constantly looking to learn and grow.

For more information or support, visit www.loveursoulagency.com or contact us on 0845 129701

Remote Working
by Marilyn Devonish

Life after lockdown. There's an interesting thought and paradigm. A few short months ago the world most likely couldn't imagine the lockdown self-isolation scenario outside the confines of a Hollywood movie, yet here we all are at the time of writing, confined, and only allowed out for essentials or exercise. So where do we begin with post pandemic society, and upon what we would base those assumptions?

I have been a Flexible Working Implementation Consultant since 2003, which means going into organisations to implement smart, flexible, and remote working policies and strategies. Covering everything from consulting with architects, designers, and ergonomic specialists to redesign office spaces, through to scoping and procurement of technology solutions, designing and delivering management and staff briefings, training sessions, and workshops, and offering Executive Coaching to support the psychology and mindset of transitioning to new ways of working.

The current situation started with doubling down on our sense of humanity, compassion, kindness, patience, and navigating the unknown. The uncertainty potentially continues as the corporate giants of the world; from Amazon to Ford, openly say they have no long-term plan or firm strategy because we are living in unprecedented times, and there's no blueprint which extends beyond a few weeks.

In this Chapter we will explore some of the biggest challenges which arise working at home, what you can do to both resolve them, and optimise your time and productivity, thus enabling the longer-term transition into remote working.

The Time Warp

When people work from home for the first time there is often a sense of euphoria; no need to get up at the crack of dawn, no commuting, no braving the elements, it's what I call the WFH Honeymoon Period. Around week three, many hit a stage where the days have no beginning nor end, and everything blends into one continuous stream, and when someone asks what day it is, you double check your calendar to be sure. There can then come a time where you are crawling the walls and not sure which way to turn. It can also affect your sleep patterns and dreams; my dream analysis article for The Express Newspaper is available via my website.

Even if you don't go as far as getting up at the same time, once you're up, add structure to your day:

- Set a schedule/agenda.
- Stop for regular breaks, including lunch.
- Finish work at a set time.
- If you're not someone who works at the weekend, honour it; make time for relaxation, no work, catching up with family and friends, etc.

Guilt

It sounds like an odd piece to include however many people feel guilty working from home if they are not doing something every single second or finish their allocated tasks early.

I always ask my Executive Coaching clients to stop and think about this one. On a regular day in the office a lot of time is often spent walking around, to and from your desk, to the filing cabinet, to the restroom, to the kitchen, to the photocopier, etc. If you broke down the intricacies, you are rarely working every single second.

When you also factor in the lack of commuting, and reduced social interaction, it makes sense you will accomplish more in a shorter timeframe. If the work has been scoped correctly, when you're finished, it is a cause for celebration rather than guilt. You know at the core of your being when you've been wasting time rather than being productive, so keep a clear perspective of the two.

NeuroSuccess™ Coaching Question: *How do you know when you've done a good job?* Also think back to any appraisals and 360 reports to ensure your view of self is objective.

Mistrust

A major downside of working from home is it being a euphemism for slacking, watching cat videos, and daytime TV. There are also times where the organisation doesn't trust the employees when they are out of sight.

Remote working during the pandemic was understandably implemented backwards; ordinarily you would scope and plan the work first, equip staff with what they need, provide briefing and training sessions, with remote working being the last step. In response to lockdown, self-isolation came first, with little or no time to plan.

Decide with your manager what needs to be done and do it. If there are set deadlines, adhere to them. The minute you realise this won't be possible, report back and say so and explain why.

Trust is earned in these situations, so to avoid the nightmare of micromanagement, start building in transparency from day one. Lack of trust can also stem from poor leadership development, an issue which demands to be handled organisationally if the arrangement is to be successful.

NeuroSuccess™ Coaching Question: *What can you do to build transparency into the working relationship?*

Work-Life Balance

Working remotely offers a glimpse of the often elusive work-life balance because it affords you time and flexibility to be there for other life events such as school plays, taking deliveries, doctor's appointments. The unfortunate flip side is when your job takes over and your home feels like an extended workplace.

To avoid this, I suggest the demarcation of spaces. If you do not have a dedicated office and are working on your kitchen table, the sofa, or in your bedroom, at the end of the working day, reclaim the area. Tidy up and clear everything away. The ritual of getting the paperwork out can be the way you mark the start of each working day.

Wherever you're working, when finished, leave the space like you would your physical office, with no going back until the next working day.

Productivity

A common problem raised with remote working is: Are you doing enough? Individuals often ask themselves this question, and many bosses are thinking it. Not solely an employee issue, this is related to how good corporate processes, systems, and procedures were before lockdown or embarking upon home working. If tasks were not accurately scoped and measured in pre-lockdown, it should be a priority now, particularly if remote working will become part of the organisational culture.

Identify KPIs (Key Performance Indicators) and how to quantify them. Once work has been completed for the day, stop. Congratulate yourself for a job well done. Get on with the rest of your social day or evening.

NeuroSuccess™ Coaching Question: *When are you most productive?* Morning, afternoon, twilight, or evening? If it doesn't disrupt the rest of your household, practice being more in alignment with your natural biorhythms, and get the bigger or more complex tasks done during your most productive times.

Resources

Having the right resources to do the job is important. When I first started out implementing flexible and remote working polices and strategies back in 2003, the technology available now didn't exist. We had to commission mobile phones, laptops, and smart encryption keys. Now it's not so much the technology; almost everyone has a smart device in their pocket, but the Apps to do the job.

Ensure you know how to get a secure connection to the intranet, knowledge web, relevant databases, etc. You can often only do half a job if you don't have access to what you need.

NeuroSuccess™ Coaching Question: *What resources do you need to do a great job?* This can be everything from ergonomic friendly furniture or seating, good internet, through to access to relevant documentation, and decent lighting.

Personal Productivity

I suggest identifying both your learning style and problem-solving style. When you identify what this is, you can relax into the process and utilise and enjoy it rather than embroiling yourself with unnecessary stress.

There are 6 keys modalities, the most common being visual, auditory, kinesthetic (feeling), AD (self-talk). It is important to know which you are because this will determine how you best deal with organisational tasking, and how you motivate yourself and focus. For example, if you are primarily visual, and your boss sends you a long list of instructions, you could find this overwhelming and confusing. An easier process for you would be to see a video walkthrough, or a one-page infographic.

NeuroSuccess™ Coaching Question: *What is your preferred learning style?* If you are not sure how to identify it, I have created a short online quiz which is available via my Flexible Working website.

Proof of Work

There is often a feeling you should be performing every second when you're working at home. I remind both employers and employees that thinking and mental planning is a valid part of both the productivity and creative process. You rarely think about thinking when you're at work because everyone can see you and therefore, you're technically working. When sat on your sofa seemingly doing nothing, this can induce guilt and panic.

NeuroSuccess™ Coaching Question: *How do you know when something is complete?* Sounds like an odd and somewhat obvious question, if the task is to close x number of calls. For more subjective tasks, the danger with being in isolation is the constant tweaking, and adding, and revising, driven by the fear of proving your worth. Identifying your completion process criteria links to the personal productivity question about your learning style because the same modalities come into play.

Boundaries

One myth of working from home is that you're not working, and therefore available at any time, including taking unsolicited calls or visits from family, friends, neighbours, or passing sales organisations.

Set boundaries, particularly if your family are also at home during the day and it disturbs your flow and concentration. Don't take unsolicited calls or allow people to pop in for impromptu chats. In the same way people most likely wouldn't dream of turning up at your office unannounced and expect you to drop everything, the same holds true for working from home.

NeuroSuccess™ Coaching Question: *How will you politely and firmly communicate and enforce your boundaries?*

Get Dressed

If you were one of the thousands of people thrust into this situation because of the coronavirus pandemic, self-isolation, and lockdown, and are new to working at home, particularly if you come from an environment where you get dressed for work, as opposed to a 'dress down Friday' approach, I recommend getting dressed even though you are at home.

It has both a physical and psychological 'uniform' effect, and acts as an anchor; think "power dressing" for those who were around in the 1980s. That's not to suggest you don a full suit and tie, more a reminder that what we wear can impact how we feel, so if sweatpants and a tee shirt don't put you in a professional mood, get dressed wearing something which does.

NeuroSuccess™ Coaching Question: *What is your version of productive power dressing?* Put the outfit on whenever you want to be at your most focused or productive.

Measure of Outputs

One problem and downside of being at home is having no "off" switch. It is easy for days to blend and lose track of time. In the absence of official KPIs, an excellent starting point is to revert to old-fashioned SMART goals and objectives.

> **S**- What specifically do you want to achieve today/this week?
>
> **M** – How you will you measure you have achieved your outcome? What is your output criteria?
>
> **A** – Is your outcome achievable?
>
> **R** – Is your outcome or objective realistic?
>
> **T** – Timing. When do you want to achieve the outcome by?

Use this as a framework for checking your progress and achievement, and for knowing when it is time to stop.

NeuroSuccess™ Coaching Question: *How many ways are there to do the job?* My mother had a saying it was: *"My way or the highway"* and this is often what it's like in the office, for example, when writing a report, you sit down all day and write the report. When working remotely, it may suit you better to write in stages, or spend half the day home-schooling, and the evening writing. The key focus here is the final outputs. If the report is completed to the required standard, it's useful to identify your optimum way of working, even if that isn't how you traditionally work in the office.

Team Spirit

Many hadn't noticed how much they value their co-workers, even those they previously classed as annoying. Those daily, what I call 'micro contacts' make up a vast amount of our day and social interactions. Lockdown and self-isolation highlighted the important role they play in our lives.

You can still maintain a sense of team spirit and collaboration whilst working remotely, it just requires a tad more creativity.

NeuroSuccess™ Coaching Exercise: List 10 ways and activities you can use to keep in touch with team members and colleagues.

Communication

It sounds cliché, but communication is key because it is easy to become isolated, stuck, lonely, confused, and even a little bored and stir crazy because we lack the usual social interactions and cues surrounding us.

Make full use of the technology at your disposal; phone, text, WhatsApp, Messenger, emails, Facetime, Skype, etc? If you are struggling, set up regular check-in sessions, either with your boss, or an accountability buddy. Lockdown has highlighted the importance of human connection by taking it all away. There as yet isn't a complete substitute for face-to-face human communication and connection, technology however can bring us several steps closer, so get scheduling.

NeuroSuccess™ Coaching Question: *What is your preferred medium of communication?* As well as making more use of it, also be open to meeting others where they're at.

Children

If you are combining working from home with childcare, rather than fight against it, or continually look for ways to work around them, identify how to make them into the process. Ideas shared with previous clients include:

1. Get children to help with putting things away and filing.
2. Create a set reading or writing space, so you are all doing the same activity for a set amount of time.
3. A race against the clock to see who can finish their work or task first.
4. Play the Silent Game when you're on the phone or a webinar, with a prize awarded to whoever stays quiet the longest.
5. Drawing and writing competitions.

NeuroSuccess™ Coaching Exercise: Come up with 10 or more ideas to engage your children and have them on standby.

Emotional Health and Wellbeing

Comments I've seen from those working from home for the first time include:

> *"I'm climbing the walls." "I don't know what day it is anymore." "I'm starting to hate the sounds of my partner breathing!" "We've not seen our kitchen table for weeks, it's buried under piles of paper." "Oh gosh, not ANOTHER Zoom meeting; my eyes are going square." "My sleep patterns are all over*

the place and the days and nights just blend into one." "I'm going stir crazy." "It seems like I'm working all the time." "I've lost the separation between work life and home life. At least at work I could get up and leave the office."

There's often a cycle associated with working from home.

Phase 1: Shock and not quite knowing what to do or how to handle it.

Phase 2: What I call the *"Woooooo whooooo"* excitement of not having to get up at the crack of dawn and commute every day.

Phase 3: This usually kicks in around week 3 once the honeymoon period and excitement is over, and a form of time distortion sets in where it becomes more challenging to distinguish what day it is, and people start climbing the walls. This phase can continue indefinitely if you don't put plans and strategies in place.

Phase 4: This is where with planning and orientation you create your sense of rhythm and flow.

I have been a Life and Executive Coach and Multi-Disciplinary Therapist since October 2000. The subject of mental and emotional health and wellbeing is vast and would require several volumes in its own right. Below is process for dealing with confusion, lack of focus, and overwhelm, which are some of the most common emotions people deal with when working from home.

Dealing with Overwhelm

A favourite modality for the majority of my clients is Huna; an ancient Hawaiian self-empowerment system. There's a process I call the Waking Meditation, which is a combination of Huna and PhotoReading™ Accelerated Learning, an extract of which is below:

1. Take a deep breath in and exhale. Breathe in through the nose and out through the mouth and naturally relax your breathing.
2. Imagine your field of vision and awareness is opening up and expending; even though you are looking straight ahead, you have a sense of what is going on around you on the periphery of your awareness; this helps engage left and right brain integration which in turn allows you to think more clearly and be more creative.
3. Metaphorically place a tangerine or point of light approximately 6 inches above your head and imagine leaving it floating there in mid-air. Trust me on this one, my clients with dyslexia and dyspraxia notice instant improvements with the full process, and those without it find their focus and concentration improves.
4. Decide what you will focus on next, in PhotoReading terms we call this your Purpose.
5. Take a deep breath in. Exhale, and if you've had your eyes closed, open your eyes, and focus on the next task.

NeuroSuccess™ Coaching Question: *How do you feel about working from home, and what are your most dominant thoughts?* If they are less than positive, work on those issues upfront otherwise they tend to sabotage the process. Even when someone is experienced in their role, a lack of confidence can creep in because you are working in a completely different environment without the traditional support systems. Rather than have it feel like you can't do "anything", identify what specifically you're having trouble with and search for a solution to that.

Motivation and Inspiration

Beyond the practicalities, logistics, and scoping the work, a lot of the success of working from home and remotely comes from mindset, motivation, and inspiration.

I distinguish between motivation and inspiration. The myth is you need to be motivated to get yourself moving and working when you are not under the watchful glare or scrutiny of a manager. To an extent this is true, particularly if you are externally referenced, meaning you work best when there is something, someone, or a deadline to push you, it does however mean you require a constant outside force to coerce or gee you on. If you can reach the stage of inspiration, the entire process becomes far easier, and sustainable in the long term because inspiration comes from within and pulls rather than pushes you.

NeuroSuccess™ Coaching Question: *Who or what motivates and inspires you?*

About the author

Marilyn Devonish, The NeuroSuccess™ Coach is the Founder of TranceFormations™, a Coaching, Training and Consultancy organisation committed to creating impactful and lasting rapid transformation and change. She has been a Flexible Working Implementation Consultant since 2003. She holds a Business Degree, Post Graduate Marketing Diploma with the Chartered Institute of Marketing, and is a Management Consultant, Prince2 Project Manager, and Change Management Specialist.

She is also a Certified Life and Executive Coach, Certified PhotoReading™ Accelerated Learning Instructor, Certified Trainer of NLP, Keynote Speaker, Off and Online Workshop Facilitator, Freelance Writer, and Certified Multi-Disciplinary

Therapist. A Personal Trainer for Your Brain, Marilyn blends aspects of neuroscience with personal development to make accelerated performance and mindset changes more easily accessible to all. She has been a Coach and Therapist since October 2000, and delivering Coaching, Training, and Therapy Sessions Online since 2005, working with both individuals and organisations to help unlock and accelerate their performance and potential.

Coaching Website: https://www.tranceformationstm.com

Email: marilyn@tranceformationstm.com

Flexible Working Website: https://flexibleworking.brizy.site/

Additional Fact Sheets on remote working are available to download from my Flexible Working Website.

Self-Awareness During Difficult Times
By Steve Hoblyn

Self-Checks

I am curious to know if you have experienced any of the following in your life, whether before, during "lockdown", or since: anger, fear, sadness, joy, difficulty in thinking clearly, lacking purpose or motivation, misunderstanding those around you, calm and in control, peaceful, well resourced?

This chapter hopes to give a few insights into all these and more and perhaps assist you in being resourced to understand this.

Awareness is and of itself curative - Fritz Perls

In this first section we will take on the first task of checking in on yourself (and of course this works for others as well).

The stress container, or life container (Fig.1.) as I refer to it is a staple in mental health awareness training and hopefully you will come to see why. This model is often reduced to a "flow" model, one where stuff goes in at the top and said stuff flows through and out at the bottom, or in this case through a tap. But like many things in life we can make this more complex and therefore more akin to our reality and experiences. Let's start:

Fig.1. The Life Container

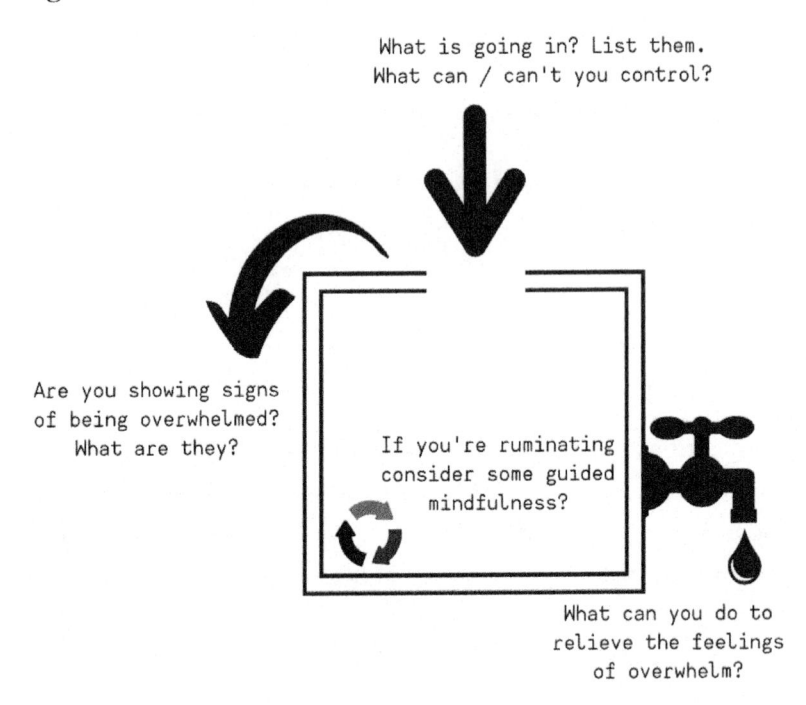

What is going in? List them.
What can / can't you control?

Are you showing signs
of being overwhelmed?
What are they?

If you're ruminating
consider some guided
mindfulness?

What can you do to
relieve the feelings
of overwhelm?

Firstly we are all of differing sizes so there is no value in comparing ourselves to others, our life experiences (protective factors and risk factors) may well determine how much we can hold with the narrative being that the more protective factors we have experienced the larger our container and the corollary being true too where more risk factors are associated with a smaller container. Please take this for what it is, a model, a way of thinking.

Next our container fills up with our minute to minute experiences; those experiences that cause us some stress. They could be smaller everyday things like something not working as it should whatever that might be, or it might be big things like trauma, loss, abandonments, failures, conflict. And it could be all the other stuff in between. It all goes in.

When we fill up, we can experience this in many ways, generally we might have a sense of unease, we might feel discombobulated. When we overflow then people will notice. A phrase given to this is a stress signature, suggesting that we all have a unique way of expressing our "overflow", you might also hear snapping-point, or overwhelm, or perhaps many other things. At this point our coping mechanisms, the through flow, is out of balance. Have a think about you and those people you know well. Do you and them have particular behaviours that are displayed when overflow happens? Who gets snappy, who withdraws into themselves, who has outbursts of other emotions? Knowing how we react, and how others react is one of the best ways to know when someone has quite frankly had enough and is in need of some support. But of course, this is at the extreme end of the spectrum and we'd rather manage the flow without ever getting to that 11/10 point.

Before we talk about the "tap" there are a couple of other nuances to consider. The first is that stuff lives in our container. Things that may have been there a long while, the sediment. When you sit and write a list of all the things in your container which is a good practice to get into, I'd suggest, you will note some things that are your historic big things. These might be the traumas, losses, upsets of your past, they sit there and ruminate, they can wake you and bother you in the night and bubble up when you're tired perhaps. These are things that may in time work their way out of the "tap", they may break down and fit through the spout, but that may take time and what you might need is to find the strength to lift them back out of the top, take them to a specialist who can help you break them down into smaller pieces.

They still go back into your container at the end of the session, but they get smaller each time and hopefully sooner rather than later they will pass.

The other things that may be in our sediment are things that are not actually ours! These are the things we pick up and hold for people who for whatever reason at the time needed us to hold something, some secret, some trauma, some experience for them as they didn't have capacity or resource to hold it themselves. When you spot these it can be quite a revelation, you might not even have realised they weren't yours, you'd been holding them for so long. For these things it might not be appropriate or timely to give them right back, but acknowledging with yourself and that person that your container has things in it which aren't yours is important. We all have agency (the ability to make our own choices and decisions, and we own these). Then when appropriately resourced and ready we should take back ownership of our own stuff. Only then can we start the work of returning these things to their rightful owners; carefully and respectfully.

So, once we know we have a container, what goes into it and how full we are, we then have greater awareness and therefore control over it. Having a regular flow out of the tap is useful to maintain a balance. Everyone should get enough sleep and eat nutritiously, that's a given. Most people also do things that they enjoy and relieves some of the pressure in their container.

- It might be exercise,
- It might be giving of their time in a volunteering capacity,
- It might be learning new things,
- It might be mindful activities or things that give them pleasure,
- It might also be connecting with other people.

These five broad categories are known as the Five Ways to Wellbeing[1]. Some may do many different things in one category and have none of the others, and some people may have a mix. Broadly speaking these will help to release the pressure in our containers. However, there are things we might think help but in excess may become blockers; you can guess what some of these might be but they could include overuse or overconsumption of social media, alcohol, drugs, foods, caffeine and other stimulants, gambling and even retail therapy and sex. The list can go on. Only you know what really helps and what doesn't. We are all unique.

A couple of other nuances to name are lids and sieves. As you'll note from the Five Ways to Wellbeing, connecting with others is one of the categories. However, there are times where we might need to disconnect, and that's fine too. Unless we're masters in meditative techniques, we may find it hard to disconnect from ourselves, however disconnecting from others by putting a lid on our container, or being more selective of our connections by using a sieve is well worth considering. If you can fashion a rudimentary lid or sieve for your container that could be worth some effort.

The final point to note, and this is an extreme situation, is that image for me from a 1990's disaster movie where the meteor is approaching Earth and it risks an "ELE"; an Extinction Level Event. These are the things we rarely see coming, and however full or empty our container, however good our tap, our lid, our sieve, the impact of this ELE meteor is enough to overflow in such an extreme way that we question our own continued existence. This is an extreme crisis situation and needs a rapid response team that

---

[1] https://neweconomics.org/2011/07/five-ways-well-new-applications-new-ways-thinking

we will not be resourced to manage ourselves, we may also be like many of those characters in the films, be in complete denial that it is happening. If this ever happens to you, please seek out help immediately.

The container therefore can be a really powerful model to keep in mind as a measure for you, and also for those around you. Very early on in lockdown I sat with my two boys who were 10 and 8 years old at the time and we did our containers together. It was not just an exercise in parent-child connection, but a practical intervention that we could draw on should we get too full whilst locked in together.

The other exercise we did together is a simple understanding of our core emotions. The movie Inside Out might be useful to watch at this point.

Emotions

You may have seen Emotion Wheels, you may have seen the Pixar movie Inside Out[2], you may be from a school of thought that our core emotions number to 4, to 6, to more or less. For the purposes of this and my work I use four; Joy, Sadness, Anger, and Fear and I will cover them briefly here in terms of one way of thinking about what they are, what triggers them, and how we can approach resolution.

The first thing to note is that a core emotion is felt in the moment; therefore, we can cycle between core emotions really rapidly. I can conceivably experience all four within a few seconds, so imagine the emotional rollercoaster we will experience throughout the day.

---

[2] https://www.pixar.com/feature-films/inside-out

Joy

Joy is that feeling of satisfaction, of being happy. Being in the moment, one where we are doing something we enjoy and are engaged with, so much so that when it comes to an end, we are conscious of thinking "where did the last half hour go?". Flow theory from Mihaly Csikszentmihalyi[3] in 1975 lends itself to this. That time where the challenge and our skill are in balance. Mindfulness practices are at play here too and we are just observing, we are not getting caught up and carried along by memories of the past or worries for the future. It sometime helps me as well to consider the other emotions at this time; if I am not feeling Anger, Sadness or Fear, then Joy as a state of contentment, being at peace or calmness is what it must be. Not the most positive approaches perhaps, however if you've struggled to identify happiness in your life as I struggled with for most of mine, knowing that just the absence of the other emotions can bring a sense of calm. It can be a starting point in explaining Joy for those that are in need of such a springboard to understanding.

When we sense Joy then there is no need to resolve it, we can just experience it, at this time it may be good to find someone or something to share it with too.

Sadness

Sadness comes from loss. So, if I lose something, someone, then sadness is a legitimate emotion to experience in that moment. We lose many things; we lose people, we lose things, we lose aspects associated with our identity, we lose time (if we ever had time to

---

[3] Mihály Csíkszentmihályi (1975). Beyond boredom and anxiety. Jossey-Bass Publishers.

lose but that's another debate). Yes, we lose many things. Sometimes we are told that we must be happy because we have gained something else in return; a promotion, a spouse, parenthood, freedom from something; but to gain we have also lost, so sadness is understandable and expected at these times too (whether societal norms agree or not). This is not about experiencing Joy and Sadness simultaneously, although you may well cycle between them. More-so that we have a Sadness relating to the past, something we have no longer.

In lockdown we lost a great deal; our freedoms, our loved ones, our work environment and colleagues, our livelihoods, our social networks, our fitness, physical contact, and in many cases perhaps a sense we've lost our minds. As a collective we have also lost hundreds of thousands of people from the planet and a sense of what was normal.

When we experience sadness, we need consolation, we need someone or something to console us, to put that proverbial arm around us and see us for who we are and what we are experiencing. The thing we've lost we might find again, or we might not. Acceptance of what is, is important.

Anger

Anger is a thing of great wonder for me. Many of us grow up misunderstanding anger, thinking of it as something not permitted or as something bad or negative. It took me a while to understand the mechanisms of anger and the huge potential for change and growth that it affords us. It also took me a long time to accept and experience it and not be scared or embarrassed by it. At its simplest anger is just energy for change. We need anger at times to motivate us, to light a fire in us about something we simply do not agree with. Anger is caused by the crossing of boundaries.

Someone or something does something that we do not believe is right according to our own values or belief system. This generates an energy in us that wants to correct this boundary or territory infringement.

The resolution is to use this energy to change something. It may be just acknowledging that a boundary has been crossed. It may mean speaking to the person about your boundary and how they crossed it, probably unknowingly as these are often invisible boundaries. Sometimes it can be a bit of a wake-up call for us to review the boundary and think more deeply about it; is it a real boundary or am I just holding it because my parents, culture, environment, workplace or other influencer "gave" the boundary to me.

Guilt is a great one for this as we can think about Guilt as anger turned inwards on oneself. In this sense we feel guilty because we have gone against our own internal belief system. We might be trying to be parent and worker and spouse and all-round good person and during lockdown realised that this was simply not possible, despite a strong internal belief that we can be all things to all people. When we realise we can't then we are angry that we have broken this belief and we experience this idea of guilt. We can attempt to resolve it by recognising what it is we believe to be true about ourselves (our boundary) and what is realistic, and give ourselves (or get from an external source) permission to relax or readjust this boundary for the new reality. Cue the "lockdown guilt" experienced by so many people.

Fear

Fear comes as a response to threat. If there is a real threat, then the legitimate emotional response in that moment is Fear. Those that have experienced this in their lives will know the psychological, physical and behavioural responses to this threat stimulus. Our heads can go into a fog, our sympathetic nervous system takes over and we elicit the fight or flight response. Our body gets prepared to defend itself. For people with anxiety they experience this often, however either without a current threat stimulus, or alternatively the reaction is out of proportion or longer than the threat would normally warrant. In regard to external threats or at least perceived threat it is real and significant. The language, imagery, timing, colour palette choices used by the authorities are cleverly planned to concentrate and focus this threat stimulus further so if you feel or felt in a constant emotional state of Fear there is a reason. It is therefore natural and ok to feel Fear at this. Fear whether from a real threat, or a false threat which appears real, is still a threat which will elicit a legitimate Fear emotion.

When we experience Fear, we need reassurance. Reassurance that we are, or will be, ok. Reassurance that the threat will pass. Hence much of the language around "This too will pass", and the sense of hope that social media, our groups and our leaders have attempted to pass onto us.

Substitute Emotions

It is worth spending a brief moment on another highly complex nuance; that of substitute emotions. The reason for touching on this is that many of you will have been exposed to Emotion Wheels (if you haven't just Google them) which give all the variations around language associated with emotion you could think of. The question we need to ask is what are you really feeling? When my kids experience an emotional response I will ask them to identify the trigger; loss, boundary infringement, threat, in order that we can truly identify the core emotion and then we can aim to "solve" it. Substitute emotions simply are when we unconsciously use one emotion to cover up for another. We are very practiced at this and it can cause huge problems as we may "solve" it in the wrong way. Think back perhaps to childhood where a sibling or school friend took a toy from you and whilst circulating between feeling Sadness from loss and Anger at having something stolen (crossed boundaries); an adult tells you it is good to share and that you should be feeling Joy about it! As adults you can perhaps see people consoling themselves for Sadness, when it is actually Anger and they more appropriately need to be addressing a crossed boundary instead. Perhaps they console themselves with retail therapy, alcohol, food etc and nothing changes. Out of awareness they are solving the wrong emotion.

An area to be mindful of is where an emotion is so extreme or out of proportion with the situation; this is a red flag, a warning that the emotion is covering up for the true emotion. The extreme outburst is perhaps a cover up for an emotion they have learned they are not allowed to feel or express. When I think back over my life, Anger as I've mentioned was an emotion I learned was not appropriate within my family culture, so it manifested as Sadness; deep Sadness for me resulted in leading a life with chronic depression. Understanding emotions and substitute emotions was a key leap forward in my recovery. For other's think perhaps also of where Sadness may not be "permitted" so it manifests as frustration, guilt or some other synonym of Anger.

Going back and reflecting on the root cause, identifying the resulting core emotion, and then attempting the appropriate resolution is a useful rule of thumb going forwards.

Needs

In his work on Transactional Analysis, Eric Berne[4] in the 60 and into the 70's wrote a great deal about our "Hungers". Our psycho-biological needs that we have as human beings. He named a few more than the three I'm about to go into detail on, but these are important ones for these times and have often been described in differing ways in lockdown articles and advice sheets.

Berne talked in terms of Structure, Recognition and Stimulus.

Structure

Our need for structure has been highlighted by Submarine Captains, Space Station Astronauts and others who have been in enforced lockdown situations. We should structure our day they say. Having spoken about this to hundreds of people during lockdown it is clear that we all have a different definition of structure but even those who say they do not need structure invariably turn out to have a form of structure in their lives.

Some had a chronological daily plan, others a list of things they hoped to achieve in the day or the week. Some though held their structures rigidly, like clinging to a life raft, and for these people the structure, if not achieved or adhered to, could become a stick with which to beat themselves with and in so doing could make things worse. So, find a way as best as possible to create a structure that works for you, and then hold it lightly, let it sway in the wind knowing the roots are secure. Or like those earthquake proof buildings in Japan that are designed to move as the

---

[4] Berne E (1972) What do You Say After You Say Hello. Grove Press

architects know that rigid structures are more fragile than lightly held structures when disturbed by external forces.

Recognition

This is a significantly sized topic, so the plan is just to brush the surface, albeit it hopefully meaningfully on this one. We all need to be seen, to exist, to be recognised for who we are. A way to think about this is the recognition we get from others, and the recognition we can afford ourselves.

When we receive recognition from others it lands for us if it is spoken in a language we understand, and less so or not at all if it's a language we don't understand. If we speak different languages to our loved ones the potential for conflict and misunderstanding are significant. This is the work that Gary Chapman[5] has done with his The 5 Love Languages. He talks about the five being:

1. Physical Touch
2. Words of Affirmation
3. Quality Time
4. Receiving Gifts
5. Acts of Service

It is a really worthwhile exercise, more so in times of isolation or separation with or from loved ones and colleagues that we understand how we need to be given recognition and work out ways to achieve this. Which of the five are the most important ones to us, and likewise what about the needs of others in our lives?

---

[5] Chapman, G. (2010). The 5 Love Languages: The Secret to Love That Lasts. Northfield Press.

Internal recognition isn't something that a lot of people seem to know or worry about. When I ask groups about gratitude diaries I am lucky to get one or two hands go up, most ask me what I mean. If people go through a therapeutic journey, sometimes with Cognitive Behavioural Therapy (CBT) but not necessarily, they may well be introduced to gratitude journaling which emerged from the Positive Psychology movement. Many children in schools have, for the current generation at least, been given these as well as part of their schooling. The format is a variation on the theme of identifying three things that they are grateful for today. And do this before going to bed. It could be the things that made you smile, that you learnt, that you've got better at. There are apps for it, there are journals like The HappySelf Journal[6] (others are available) for kids and teens (and therefore by default adults!). Gratitude journaling rewires us to be more positive.

If we have lost out on getting external recognition, then we will always have ourselves who can in part at least meet some of this need.

Stimulus

Too much or too little stimulus we will touch on later, but getting the right amount can motivate us, keep us interested and engaged, and curious about the world around us. The behavioural psychologists might talk in terms of us being creatures of stimulus-response. We are constantly responding to a stimulus. Hunger elicits eating. Tiredness elicits sleeping. Emails elicit a response too. Social media user interfaces elicit infinite scrolling as the stop stimulus was removed by clever designers.

---

[6] https://happyselfjournal.com

It is important to maintain a Goldilocks balance of stimulus and be mindful of when it is becoming too much, or too little. More on this later.

Resources

To weather any storm we need the right resources, and perhaps equally if not more important is that we need to feel well resourced.

> There's no such thing as bad weather, only unsuitable clothing
>
> — Alfred Wainwright

During recent events, and I suppose throughout life, we are all in the same storm but not in the same boat. A poem along the same vein also did the rounds during lockdown (reproduced in the Appendix). It may be the same storm; however, we are all experiencing different aspects of it and the resources (the boat, supplies, skill sets, crew, direction, and even purpose at being out at sea) are all different. Some had already weathered smaller storms; some had never seen anything but sunny landlocked days. And of course, everything in between.

When we think about our resources it might be helpful to grab a piece of paper and a pen and draw a horizontal line across it as in Fig.2. In the space above the line list out all those resources you have available to you in the external environment. Friends, family, colleagues, social network, clubs, hobbies, assets and tangible goods. Once you have drawn all these you might see some clusters, some groupings, things that you might use as resources for one situation or context but not another. Friends you would see for fun, others you might reach out to in times of distress.

You might see some gaps emerging, you might reflect on times gone by when you needed an external resource but did not have the right one to hand. You might have since filled those gaps. Reflect on what you see.

Below the line is for your internal resources. Whereas the external resources will ebb and flow, come and go, grow and shrink, the internal resources will only ever continue to grow. Every experience, every challenge, every first attempt in learning (f.a.i.l.), every training course, every therapy session, every mentor, role model, memory and mantra sit here. Most will be outside of your consciousness but as you start to write and reflect, the enormity of your own resources will come flooding into sight.

This is a living document. Add and subtract from it, play with it and enjoy it. Draw on it when you need to feel resourced.

Fig.2. Resourcing Ourselves

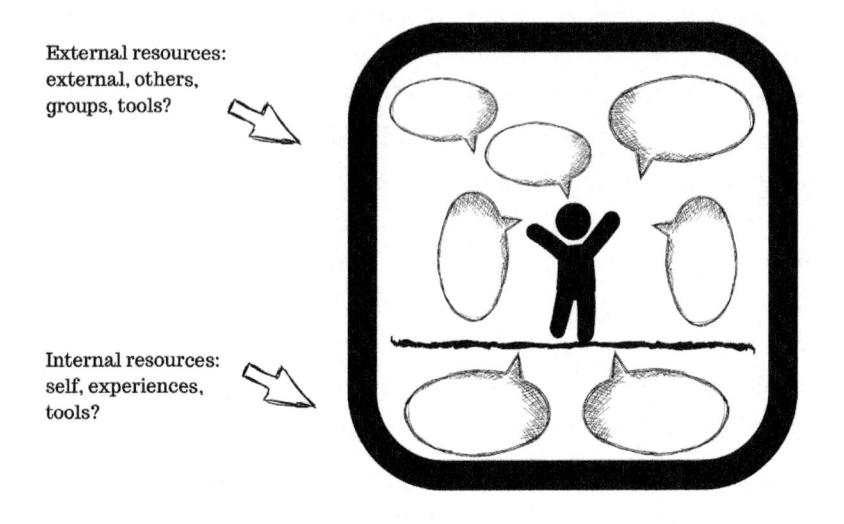

External resources: external, others, groups, tools?

Internal resources: self, experiences, tools?

Our strengths are a huge internal resource available to us as well. When I began my career the talent model used in business was predominantly a development based one; we cared little about people's strengths, they were a given, however peoples' areas in need of development were hugely significant. These powered a whole series of annual processes and fed the daily grind of trainer's workloads both internal and specialist external consultants. Over the last few years there has been a shift in some quarters towards a more strengths-based approach. About time too. We will never all be the same and the stress caused by chasing the impossible is unhelpful to our wellbeing, but working to our strengths, now that's got something hugely positive around it.

In our work around coping with adverse times, knowing our resources and our strengths is very powerful. Using a Strengths based questionnaire[7] we were able to identify someone's top 5 strengths (from a universally identifiable list of 25). On reading their key strengths, people's reactions were commonly of two types: the first was that they went to bed with a smile on their face, the other was that they skim read through them looking for their development areas (which of course there weren't any). This tells us a few things but perhaps mainly how hard wired we are to feel the benefit of recognition (see Needs) and also how our wiring extends to expecting to be told we're not good enough as we are (hence the rise in CBT therapy to help disavow us of this false belief).

Once people have their list of strengths they can be used, like putting on a pair of much needed glasses, to see the world around us, our immediate environment, in a way we might not have before. For those that have strengths around seeing beauty,

---

[7] https://strengthsbasedresilience.com/assessments/ssq72

the appearance and design of their environment is of key importance. For those that have creativity you begin to understand how they find motivation in finding new ways of doing things. For those who have leadership as a strength, they will have found a way of using this during lockdown and tough times and people look to them in this role. For those who have a love of learning they are perhaps more aligned to using the time to expand their knowledge and awareness. The list and opportunities to work with our strengths goes on.

Purpose

> Purpose, it's that little flame that lights a fire under your ass
>
> — Avenue Q, Purpose.

One key area that began to surface midway through lockdown was around Purpose. From one psychological perspective (Schmid 2008[8]) we are a distinct product of four different Worlds in which we inhabit multiple Roles; our Personal World, our Community World, our Organisational World and our Professional World. If you stop to draw out these four Worlds (Fig.3.) and then subdivide them into all the different Roles[9] within each, what emerges is a rich kaleidoscope of who you are and the purpose you have found for yourself, consciously or out of awareness.

---

[8] Schmid, B (2008) The Role Concept of Transactional Analysis and Other Approaches to Personality, Encounter, and Cocreativity for All Professional Fields. Transactional Analysis Journal Volume 38, 2008 - No. 1
[9] A role is a coherent system of attitudes, feelings, behaviours, perspectives on reality, and accompanying relationships (Schmid 2008).

Fig.3. Example of Our Worlds and Roles

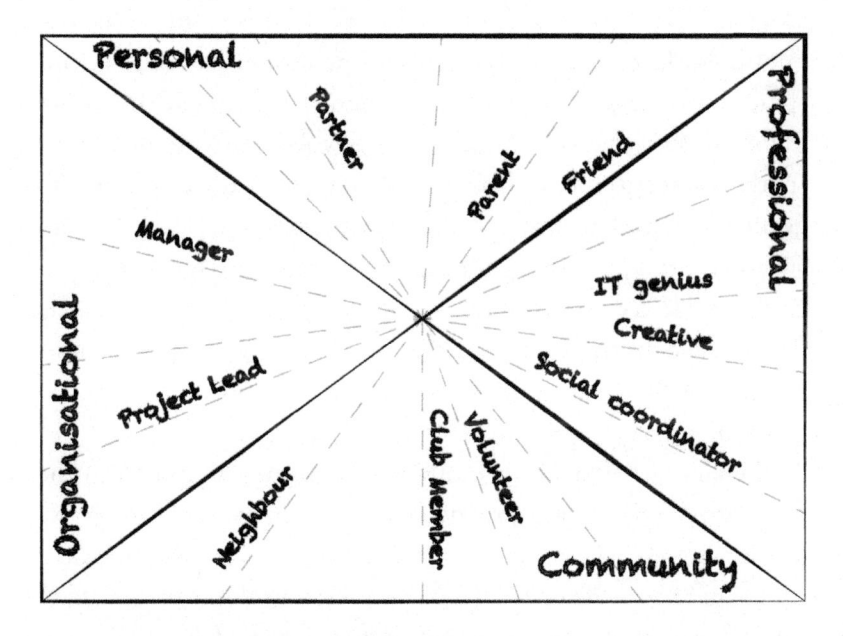

[Figure: A rectangle divided by two diagonals into four triangular sections labelled Personal (top), Professional (right), Community (bottom), and Organisational (left). Roles shown include: Partner, Parent, Friend, Manager, IT genius, Creative, Project Lead, Social coordinator, Neighbour, Volunteer, Club Member.]

- Personal: roles that make you the person you are; things you do, roles you realise, experiences you've had, values you hold about these? This could be a full section.
- Organisational: this is for the roles you realise at work; job titles and other roles you might have.
- Professional: this is for all your work-related skills and things you do, not the tiles or roles you hold.
- Community: this is for all the things you do in the community and in the wider society.

Simon Sinek (2017) talks in his books and lectures about Find Your Why[10]. The work to be done in this regard is to

---

[10] Sinek, Simon (2017). Find Your Why: A Practical Guide for Discovering Purpose for You and Your Team. New York: Portfolio/Penguin.

explore yourself internally, and with those that know in order for you to essentially identify your strengths and the areas that people look to you for. From this you should be able to construct a powerful "Purpose" statement for yourself. It's more involved than that of course and well worth reading the books. In the concepts being laid out here we can do this more in depth, and perhaps with the help of someone else who can spot gaps and patterns that might be outside of our awareness. Cross reference this with our resources and strengths from the previous sections you might find something very special shining back at you that before this time you might have been too busy to see.

Having a better idea of our Purpose not only provides the motivation (the Stimulus) we need to get us up moving and grooving, but it can also provide us a plan (Structure) and achievement (Recognition) to meet our Needs outlined in the earlier section. Of course, there are many, many other forms of Structure and Recognition beyond having a plan and a sense of achievement, a few of which are captured elsewhere in this Chapter. Finding what works for you in each context and over time is well worth a moment of your reflection time.

Clear Thinking

All of the above is well and good when we are thinking clearly and in a good place. However difficult life events, viruses, and lockdowns have a knack of knocking us off balance and fogging our heads. We begin to React Not Respond. When actually what we want to do is Respond Not React. When our container overflows we are not best placed to make big decisions, choose a direction, or even answer that email.

Everyday Hypnotic Inductions (or the things that get in the way of a clear head)

A number of key destabilisers have been identified (titled in the psychology as Everyday Hypnotic Inductions by Conway & Clarkson 1987[11]) and when you read these think about how they played out in lockdown, not just personally but with our business leaders and even the people in charge of our countries. When these happen, we do not think clearly, and as our medicinal patient information leaflets often read: Do Not Operate Heavy Machinery.

I have summarised Clarkson's list into the following seven areas, they are:

1. Extreme Emotional States
2. Lack of Control
3. Pain and Illness
4. Shock
5. Boredom and Understimulation
6. Too Much Stimulation
7. An Impossible Task.

When we look through this list and overlay it on our current situation or other times of great change you will perhaps note some issues. Firstly, we are all in an extreme emotional situation. Looking back at the core emotions let's just pick Fear. Fear of a killer virus. This induces No. 1: Extreme Emotional States. Add No. 2: Lack of Control to this then things get much harder; how

---

[11] Conway, A. & Clarkson, P. (1987) Everyday Hypnotic Inductions. Transactional Analysis Journal Volume 17, 17-23

much control do we have over an airborne virus we cannot see and little concept of how it will impact the human being it comes into contact with. Bad enough. Add in No. 6.: Too Much Stimulation. Everyone I worked with talked openly about being overwhelmed by too much information; too many offers of "support", too many channels of news, too much social media presence, too much connection, too many meetings, too many messages of "how're you doing?". If you are in a leadership position you have all of this, plus perhaps the government advisors, scientists, psychologists, the media, economists, business leader and special interest groups all bombarding you with data and opinion, most of which is also coming from a foggy head because they are just human beings as well. Now we're in difficulties aren't we if we want clear headed direction. And then you're hit with No. 7.: An Impossible Task. Well if a global crisis isn't one of those then we need to think hard about what that could mean. An Impossible Task will destabilise us instantly.

So, the message here is clear. Cut ourselves and our leaders some slack as it is very hard to do anything with these Everyday Hypnotic Inductions in play. And yet right now and during lockdown we are having to Operate Heavy Machinery, so we need to do it as safely and as slowly as possible so as few get hurt as possible.

Transitions

Another aspect that people noticed very early on was how bad they felt moving too quickly from one role to another. Think back to the Worlds in the section on Purpose and you'll remember this. It is tough enough moving from one role to another (for example parent to spouse, to friend, to sibling) within one World; in this example the Personal World. However, moving between Worlds is an even bigger gear shift. In lockdown the boundaries between these Worlds and these roles have become blurred and if we are not mindful of safe transitions, we are like a car being dumped from 5th to 2st gear for a tight hairpin without matching engine revs. Advanced drivers capable of heel-toe are aware of the importance of matching engine speeds to gear ratios hence they do an intervention; a subtle but highly important blip of the accelerator to allow higher gears to engage without locking up the wheels and causing a skid. If that analogy resonates, or not, please note that a transition between different speeds (roles) needs timing and consideration, and some element of awareness of the implications of getting it wrong or timing it badly.

When we transition between work and non-work, between being a parent, spouse, child, friend and all the other roles we have we need to acknowledge this. There are a number of ways this can be done; we can symbolically close our laptops, chime a bell, change our clothing, take a shower, wash our hands, clap, light or extinguish a candle, change rooms (side note: don't work in your bedroom is a clear message we've had consistently since school days as it impacts on our sleep). Many options are available, and you will find what works for you. But do something. In normal life we have commuting time, some form of recognisable role uniform, transition between work areas or meeting rooms. To use the above analogy that is nice sequential gearing 5th to 4th to 3rd to 2nd to 1st. Now we need to be racing drivers and perfect our heel-toe manoeuvre so we can blip our accelerator and drop 5th to 2nd or 1st to be able to take the corner safely before accelerating out into the next straight. It's great fun once mastered.

Language

Speaking the same language as others is critical to safe and smooth working, whether in the workplace or at home. If we speak different languages the analogy goes, we will speak loudly and slowly and still not be understood, just causing frustration. Remembering the section above on Needs and the Five Love Languages of our Need for Recognition, we'll recall how important this is. Frustration can lead to No. 1.: Extreme Emotional States and we React Not Respond.

Listening

In a more direct association with our understanding of language it is also important to listen to someone, truly listen, and not feel the need to give advice or opinion. We so often worry about saying the wrong thing or making things worse. I would suggest that Wrong and Worse are contextual and personal to the person, none of which we can know or predict. All we can do it listen to their story, be mindful of our judgements and opinions about it, and figure out with them what it is they might need. In most contexts just listening will be enough. In other situations there may well be something specific that is needed and we can talk about the Resources they have to meet the need. Rather than being paralysed by concerns of Wrong and Worse, our intention is the most critical. If someone senses that we genuinely care this will shine through any mess that we might make of our words.

The pursuit of active non-judgemental listening is a skill in itself and can take years to grasp, however the adage of Less is More is such an important thing to keep in mind. Less (from you) talking, less opinion, less judgement, less advice, less internal noise, less worry about getting it wrong. Just notice someone needs you and listen. See how well people of different backgrounds and languages communicate in those cultural docuseries on TV; you'll see how meaning and understanding come across purely by nature of curiosity, listening and our intention to understand.

Resilience

We have heard a great deal about Resilience over the last few years. It has become big business. Trainers and organisations are set up to provide e-learning, half day courses, and whole workbooks dedicated to understanding this phenomenon, which was once simply thought of as being "strong". Being resilient is seen as a key attribute for employees, leaders, and businesses as a whole. Consider how resilience is playing out as a result of your current context.

A delegate once said to me that resilience cannot be trained, it can only come from experiencing hardship and surviving it. Quite an anti-nod to the thousands being spent by their organisation on training in this topic. A coaching client of mine showed me his "Resilience" worksheet he'd had to complete in a half day workshop. He's never since looked at it, couldn't remember the content, and again was quite dismissive of it. A third, a colleague of mine who has been working with clients for the past decade in this space has achieved some measurable results with a client, but not through one off workshops. The achievements have been through workshops, work groups, line manager sessions, sharing of struggles and experiences, realisation that they are not alone, and supporting each other to help learn and grow from adversity.

Resilience is not now readily defined as strength with the ability to take the knocks without breaking. A concept that some people and businesses I've come across tell me they understand resilience to be. This supposes that like a steel bar, we can take knock after knock, and if we break, that's it, we are scrap metal and replaced by another girder from the pile.

Resilience has been coined as "Bouncebackability", originally it is said coming from Iain Dowie about Crystal Palace Football team;

Bouncebackability: the ability to recover quickly from a setback.

For those of us who have experienced setbacks in our lives, recovery is not always quick, but this does not detract from the experience and our building of resilience.

This definition of Bouncebackability also misses a key ingredient of resilience that the scientific understanding would include; the ingredient of change or growth. In Physical Sciences we might hear about something that has been bent out of shape then returning to its original shape, with additional kinetic and potential energy generated from its distortion. A snapshot taken when the object is bent out of shape could be mistaken for being broken, however time-lapse forward and you will see this reform itself, containing greater energy.

An important aspect then around our current thoughts of resilience is an ability over time to move to a new position having something additional to what was there before but retaining aspects of the original. This is something captured in a model and definition adapted by Rosemary Napper from Brian Walker's ideas about Resilience:

> Real resilience in individuals and organisations is the capacity to absorb disturbance to our frame of reference, reorganise and create a new identity i.e. 'a new story' which contains enough of the old to feel congruent and recognisably ourselves.

If you examine Fig. 4. with me we will see a number of important areas to consider when it comes to understanding resilience in this context and in the context of moving on from disturbing life events.

Fig. 4. Real Resilience

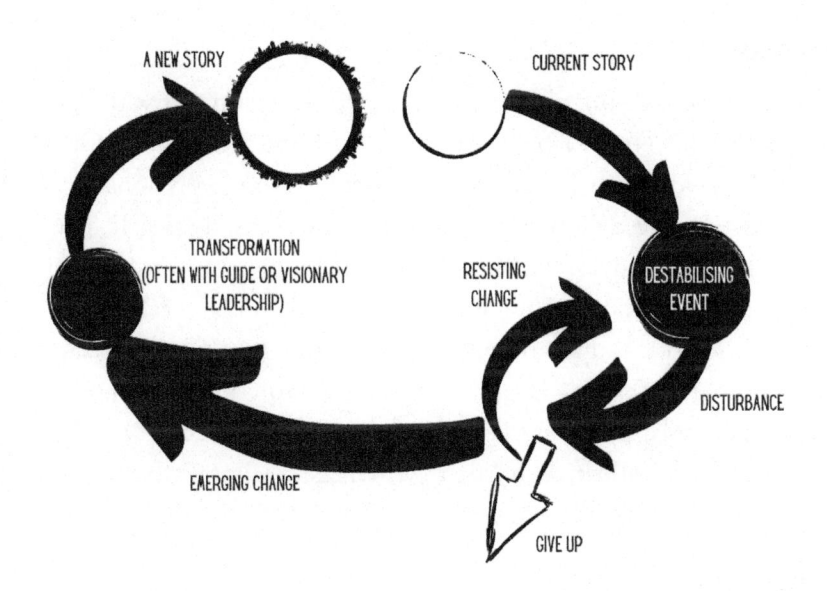

[Figure 4: Diagram showing a cyclical flow with labels: CURRENT STORY → DESTABILISING EVENT → DISTURBANCE → RESISTING CHANGE / GIVE UP → EMERGING CHANGE → TRANSFORMATION (OFTEN WITH GUIDE OR VISIONARY LEADERSHIP) → A NEW STORY]

This is a cycle that you can see playing out in our lives over and over again and sometimes overlapping disturbances can result in a serious impact on people and organisations.

If we follow the cycle through it is clear that at some point our frame of reference, our 'normal', is disturbed by a major event that rocks our world. The impact of this disturbance can manifest in a washing cycle of experiences that can hold us in a vortex of thoughts, feelings and behaviours for very long periods. This vortex has a plethora of hooks that pull us back in over and over again, as we can readily see when we ruminate over past tragedies and traumas (the coulda, woulda, shoulda thinking). This can be experienced as being at the "Edge of Chaos".

Our exit routes are threefold:

Resist

To resist the disturbance, deny it and try to reconnect with what was before. The Kubler Ross Model[12] of the 5 Stages of Grief would have this as Denial, the first stage. Although rationally we know that the disturbance has happened, we still wish to cling to what was and are unable to, and in so doing risk further feeding the disturbance. Thinking about disturbances to clear thinking above you can see how extreme emotional distress can cause havoc here. We saw this effect not necessarily in behaviour but certainly in language used during lockdown in terms of "go back to normal, "return to normal", whereas we know there is no 'back', only forward.

Give Up

Giving up is extreme and perhaps in the later adaptations to the Kubler Ross Model we might see this as Depression or Crisis. It is associated with a total loss of energy. In the five common reactions to trauma this could most closely align with the colloquialism "Flop":[13] complete dissociation from ourselves and the situation. It could even result in suicide when in extremis so should not be underestimated.

Emergence and Transformation

The third exit route leads to a new story; the place of resilience but it is not an easy path as it takes energy and often visionary

---

[12] Kubler Ross, E (1969) On Death & Dying. Simon & Schuster/Touchstone.
[13] The 5 common stages of traumatic response: 1. Friend, 2. Fight, 3. Flight, 4. Freeze, and 5. Flop.

leadership or mentorship to guide us through, and the hooks back to the disturbance and other routes still remain. It is likely that we will need to stay with feelings of discomfort for some time, even years, explore the depths of emotion and meaning, find a meaning and then a purpose. We will need to experience a paradigm shift and value change and a reorganisation of our lives. This takes huge energy and is risky but is an essential path to avoid the alternatives.

New Story

The new version of us or the organisation that emerges, if we can find that path, still retains enough of the past to be recognisable, however there is growth, renewed energy and awareness that was not there before. Additional skills will have emerged, strengthening our or its belief and energy systems to feel we can weather future disturbances, knowing that they too will come with great discomfort and challenge.

Conclusion

There has been a significant global disturbance where we can see the collapse of previous systems that are not designed or capable of sustaining a new world order. We have seen systems that try to cling to the past and deny the changes around us hoping for a return to what was before, and we see those embracing new ways to work remotely, slow their lives, focus on what is important to them, and perhaps most importantly may have been able to spend precious time with themselves learning what makes them special and unique in this world.

Working with teams and leaders over this period to give frameworks for self-understanding (and in so doing understanding of others) and following my and their rollercoaster journey has been a profoundly unique privilege. I see a world emerging where self-understanding, awareness and acceptance of our triggers, needs and differences is key to moving forwards. This event has brought greater trust from leadership. It has brought greater understanding of the multiple roles we all try to play. It has revealed the gaps in our perception of what it means to be perfect, to be strong, to try hard, and a need to please people. It has also given us a crash course in understanding resilience and the effort it takes to attain.

About the Author

Bio

Steve brings together professional, personal and his own lived experience of supporting mental ill health in the workplace. Having trained in psychology, he is a qualified and experienced executive, team and systemic coach, working as a therapeutic coach following significant training in transactional analysis counselling. He is an MHFA England Mental Health First Aid Instructor, a Suicide First Aid associate tutor, a mental health and wellbeing speaker and advocate, and an ambassador for the charity MQ. He is the co-founding member of the Association of Mental Health Advocates.

The darkest times, failures, and a troubled life have been more than balanced by the chance to work at and alongside the highest levels of world leading organisations. His corporate life spanned over 20 years, from working as a consultant in a Big 5 professional services firms, to a Reward Lead in FMCG, and an Executive Director HR role in Global Pharmaceutical.

Background

Steve's philosophy and approach has been slow cooked in the crucible of his direct experiences and many modalities of training.

Initially training in Psychology and Sports and Exercise Sciences he moved into a Postgraduate in Outdoor Education framed squarely in theories and practice of experiential learning using the outdoors.

His workplace training experiences spanning over 20 years were diverse including leadership training developed from the London School of Economics and time spent at INSEAD in France. In this time, he worked and led significant people related projects across the world with many different cultures. He qualified and still practices as an executive coach with a particular interest in teams and somatic work.

Following a serious breakdown which exposed traumatic childhood experiences that had lain dormant for 35 years he found himself in serious trouble and a period which almost took his life. Working intensely with trauma therapists, clinical psychologists, coaches, counsellors and other healing specialists from the mainstream to the off beaten track he has healed and now thrives in bringing these experiences to those who are interested in hearing more.

His return to mental health began in successfully completing the first few modules of an MSc in the Neuroscience and Psychology of Mental Health with Kings College London which he later discontinued in favour of a more practical workplace approach of mental health first aid and awareness, and focussing on deeper therapeutic counselling training in Transactional Analysis. In 2018 he began a journey with an organisation based in the Lake District to experience more about rites of passage, vision questing, and psychosynthesis.

He has been running his own business since 2016 working in a number of ways from strategy to training and support, with a number of large global household name clients.

During lockdown he shifted his focus to offer self-awareness and organisational counselling sessions virtually with staff, line managers and mental health first aider groups. In these sessions, which form the basis of this chapter, he brought together all of this to help individuals and leaders understand more about themselves so they could be better resourced in themselves to get through these new times and additionally so they could be there for others.

www.igallos.com
www.amha-uk.org
steve@igallos.com
https://www.instagram.com/findtic/
uk.linkedin.com/in/stevehoblyn

References

Berne E (1972) What do You Say After You Say Hello. Grove Press

Chapman, G. (2010). The 5 Love Languages: The Secret to Love That Lasts. Northfield Press.

Conway, A. & Clarkson, P. (1987) Everyday Hypnotic Inductions. Transactional Analysis Journal Volume 17, 17-23

Csíkszentmihályi, M (1975). Beyond boredom and anxiety. Jossey-Bass Publishers.

Five Ways to Wellbeing: https://neweconomics.org/2011/07/five-ways-well-new-applications-new-ways-thinking

Kubler Ross, E (1969) On Death & Dying. Simon & Schuster/Touchstone.

The HappySelf Journal: https://happyselfjournal.com

Schmid, B (2008) The Role Concept of Transactional Analysis and Other Approaches to Personality, Encounter, and Cocreativity for All Professional Fields. Transactional Analysis Journal Volume 38, 2008 - No. 1

Sinek, Simon (2017). Find Your Why: A Practical Guide for Discovering Purpose for You and Your Team. New York: Portfolio/Penguin.

Strengths Based Questionnaire: https://strengthsbasedresilience.com/assessments/ssq72

Appendix
WE ARE NOT IN THE SAME BOAT
Author unknown

I heard that we are in the same boat.

But it's not like that.

We are in the same storm, but not in the same boat.

Your ship can be shipwrecked and mine might not be.

Or vice versa.

For some, quarantine is optimal: a moment of reflection ,re-connection. Easy, in flip flops, with a whiskey or tea.

For others, this is a desperate crisis.

For others, it is facing loneliness.

For some, peace, rest time, vacation.

Yet for others, Torture: How am I going to pay my bills?

Some were concerned about a brand of chocolate for Easter (this year there were no rich chocolates)

Others were concerned about the bread for the weekend, or if the noodles would last a few more days.

Some were in their "home office"

Others are looking through trash to survive.

Some want to go back to work because they are running out of money.

Others want to kill those who break the quarantine.

Some need to break the quarantine to stand in line at the banks.

Others to escape.

Others criticize the government for the lines.

Some have experienced the near death of the virus, some have already lost someone from it, some are not sure their loved ones are going to make it, and some don't even believe this is a big deal.

Some of us who are well now may end up experiencing it, and some believe they are infallible and will be blown away if or when this hits someone they know.

Some have faith in God and expect miracles during 2020

Others say the worst is yet to come.

So, friends, we are not in the same boat.

We are going through a time when our perceptions and needs are completely different.

And each one will emerge, in his own way from that storm

Some with a tan from their pool. Others with scars on the soul (for invisible reasons)

It is very important to see beyond what is seen at first glance. Not just looking, more than looking, seeing

See beyond the political party, beyond biases, beyond the nose on your face. Do not underestimate the pain of others if you do not feel it.

Do not judge the good life of the other, do not condemn the bad life of the other.

Don't be a Judge

Let us not judge the one who lacks, as well as the one who exceeds him.

We are on different ships looking to survive.

Let everyone navigate their route with respect, empathy and responsibility.

Growing Happiness
by Imogen Tinkler

Is it actually possible to improve your wellbeing by being more connected with your food and the seasons around you?

This chapter will look at our relationships with food and the seasons. It will give you five ways in which you can improve your wellbeing, by making small steps that will change your behaviours and habits for a lifetime.

Each generation has become more disconnected from their local environment and the seasons around us. Around 60% of people in the UK eat the same seven meals every single week. The research commissioned by Jamaican Ginger Beer Company[14] also found that people have been eating the same meal on the same day of the week for over ten years. This absolutely blows my mind - the study concluded "we are really lacking imagination when it comes to experiences with flavours."

I wonder if it is imagination or other factors that really stop us being more experimental and varied with our food?

---

[14] Constant Berkhout, 2015. *Retail Marketing Strategy: Delivering Shopper Delight*. pp. 21 - 22.

There are millions of recipe books, cooking shows, YouTube channels and free information out there, but we stay in a place of comfort. Yet, are you really comfortable if you feel guilty for not exploring or trying different things? We lack the time, space, and confidence to really experiment - my hope is that our story will help you change that. When I was little, my parents would be so delighted when I loved something new that we would then have it every week, which for me defeated the point. Just because I love something it doesn't mean that I want to eat it every single week.

Why do we do this? Because we have lost the connection with our food, the seasons, and the outside world. We feel that we should be able to eat the same things all year round - so what if I want to eat strawberries in winter, sardines in April or lamb at Easter? We have moved from a world where we eat, into one where we consume. We don't ask what the farmer has or what's going to taste good right now, but rather we go to the supermarket, farm shop or order online with a shopping list of what we desire. If they don't supply it, we will simply get it somewhere else.

At university I lived on tuna and sweetcorn pasta and wine; apart from when I went to my friend Vikki's. Vikki would always cook something wonderful that I'd never had before, she'd cook things like stuffed marrow or bread and butter pudding. I used to think it was luxury dining. It is only now, as I build a better understanding of how food and food shopping really works, that I realise she was buying a marrow as they were only 10p because there was a huge glut of them - so it was a really cheap meal to make for herself and her friends, like me. She chose bread and butter pudding, not because it was fancy, but because she wanted to use her loaf by using up all her stale bread. She wanted zero waste.

Who are we?

We are a family of three, with a little dog Spartacus. We live by the seaside on the Kent coast, in a small but perfectly formed town called Whitstable. It is famous for its oysters, pirate alleyways and for inventing scuba diving!

As a family we moved here for three reasons

1. My father passed away and he had a holiday home here. We both grew up by the sea and missed it so much.
2. My husband, Duncan, had been struggling with his mental health and we thought the sea would help.
3. We wanted to set up our food business, Bangers and Balls here as we would be nearer suppliers and produce at the very heart of the county known as the Garden of England.

When we moved we knew no one. We had no children and were in the very early stages of setting up our own business, so it was difficult to meet people. We'd made the move, out of the city, to improve our quality of life, Duncan's mental health, and to make a real commitment to our business idea, which was in its infancy. Focusing on our food and where it came from felt like one way to embrace this new life, start our business, start our family, and make new friends as we went.

When we started to connect with small local farms, we were amazed to meet people our age - people who weren't from a farming background and still they were doing something amazing. We started to build our own community and to learn so much. Bangers and Balls - and our passion for good eating - has grown from there.

Getting creative

Our mission became eating the seasons. In part, this was a way to teach ourselves more about what we needed to know for our work. I found this a little overwhelming when we decided to start; one of my favourite foods in the world is avocado and I used to love poached eggs with avocado and chilli on toast, it set me up for the day – every day. Now, this wasn't something I could have every day, so I set myself a challenge. For 30 days I wanted to try different things - and now this excitement for the new has become part of life. I still have an avocado, but now it's only once a month and I really look forward to having it, rather than just consuming it without any thought! My challenge for creativity and inspiration for breakfast led to us starting our online Sunday Brunch Club. This helps people look forward to cooking something different for breakfast, just once a week, and we focus on helping them to use up what they have in their larder in a fun and inventive way.

Electric Daisy anyone? No, you've never heard of them either? Neither had we. Electric daisies are truly wonderful things - the first time I tried was one I was pregnant. I thought someone had given me drugs - my mouth started to fizz and pop like I had licked a battery! I wouldn't suggest eating one raw on its own, but they are a great addition to a sorbet to really bring it alive on the plate. Electric Daisies, however, are quite expensive from small local farmers, but we discovered that we could grow them at home, for just a few pounds. As we learned more and became more connected to our food and our community, I hated having to pay for things that we could grow at home. That is the honest reason we started to grow our own things, and then my whole wellbeing started to change. I found joy in watching those plants grow and sprout. I found satisfaction in knowing exactly how and where my food had grown.

Life lessons from the earth

There were further impacts too - gardening taught me that you can help plants, but you can't control them. There are lots of outside factors. Just like us as humans. Sometimes we need a little bit more love and care to bring us back to life and other times we need to be left alone.

In March 2020, we suffered one of the worst losses I think a family can ever go through. Our beautiful little girl Beatrix passed away in our arms. We had done everything to care for her, feed her and still, she hadn't survived. The pain was huge. I couldn't understand why it had happened. I felt like it must have been my fault - I mustn't have fed her enough, maybe I didn't change her nappy enough, there had to be a reason and it had to be my fault. In learning to garden, I have often looked for the reason a seed didn't grow, or a plant didn't survive - I look for the reason and I assume it's my fault. In growing my own food and in life, I have learned that sometimes there is much that is out of my control. Plants like humans can't be controlled; you can only do your best and learn as you go along.

Growing together

It was after this that we went all in and changed our garden completely. In our grief and in everything we've learned since starting on our food journey, we knew that we needed to do something to give ourselves a sense of purpose and hope in lockdown. We had lost our little girl and all our future business events had been cancelled - we usually run quirky pop up supper clubs and sustainable experiences. It felt like the world we had been working so hard to create had all been pulled from under us. We also knew we weren't alone in this. We thought - what if we could do something to bring our community together, something to help us as well as others. So, we started the Foodie Revolution. We invited 25 people to commit a few hours a week to improve their own wellbeing by making small behaviour changes. It was a small experiment based on everything we have seen and experienced as our connection to food and the seasons has grown. It would be fun, it would be different, it would be something that anyone could join in - no matter your level of green fingers. During a time of great upheaval, for our family and for others, by investing in our sense of community we could hold ourselves to account, share our knowledge, and grow food and our wellbeing together.

We had a choice to make. My mother always wanted a separate patch of garden to grow food, and I believe that Duncan and I are the only people in the history of the world to move out of London and end up having a smaller garden. For the time we've lived here we have had a lawned postage stamp size of a garden that Duncan hates mowing. Every few weeks, we would have the same argument- he likes it as a wild garden for the bees to thrive in and me saying it is only because you hate mowing and what will the neighbours think! With a little help from an Offgrid living specialist, who happens to be one of our new farming community friends, we have transformed our garden (all our garden) into a planting area. Jack instructed us not to dig the lawn, instead cover the whole area with two to three layers of cardboard - so there is no space for the grass to grow, and to put 40 - 50 bags of compost over it. Once all that was done, we could then plant our plug plants and seeds. Suddenly, with a little help from our friends, the overwhelm had gone and we could start. Jack had demystified the process for us and solved the problem by making it bite sized and easy - and this is what I offer to you too. The joy of watching our garden grow has been amazing! It was such a big thing for us to do and now I love watching and helping with the sowing of seeds, I love it even more when everything pops up - it feels rather magical!

It isn't just us who is feeling like this! The data shows (Lloyds Bank 2015)[15], that people value their gardens highly, considering the size and presence of a garden as similarly important to the size of the house. This is particularly important for parents and I wonder if this will become even more important in the coming months or years? Sales of vegetable seeds in the UK now exceed sales of flower seeds for the first time since the Second War and in 2015, sales of "grow your own veg" accounted for almost 80 percent of sales of seeds and plants compared to just 30 per cent in the 1990s[16]. Recent surveys of local authorities and their allotments confirm this increased demand (Priestly 2015)[17] Over 30 percent of local authorities that responded said that they had between 100 and 400 people waiting for plots, while 8.5 per cent had more than a 1,000 people waiting. I know the feeling, we signed up for an allotment when we first moved to Whitstable. That was four years ago and we joined the waitlist at number 35. I checked again last week to see what number we were and we are still number 35.

---

[15] Lloyds Bank, 2015, *Britain at Home Competing with computers: Parents spruce up gardens to tempt children outdoors.* https://www.dotrythisathome.com/wp-content/uploads/2015/06/Britain-at-Home-Lloyds-Bank-Insurance-03-06-15.pdf

[16] Charlotte Elizabeth Hadleyan, 2017. *Ethnographic Study of Allotmenteering: Practising Sustainability.*

[17] David Buck, 2016 *Gardens and health Implications for policy and practice* This report was commissioned by the National Gardens Scheme. https://www.kingsfund.org.uk/sites/default/files/field/field_publication_file/Gardens_and_health.pdf

Food for the soul

Well that all sounds interesting, but how do allotments and gardening relate to our wellbeing?

Research (Wood et al (2015)[18] finds that tending to a garden, at home or at an allotment, demonstrates benefits to our mood, self-esteem, and other indicators of wellbeing. What I find particularly interesting, is that the wellbeing indicators were not dependent on how long people had been gardening. A study conducted in the Netherlands by (Van den Berg and Custers 2011)[19] showed that allotment gardening was linked to decreases in measured cortisol levels and increases in positive mood, these findings were the first experimental evidence that gardening can promote relief from acute stress and boost wellbeing.

This all sounds great doesn't it, but how can you get started today in your own home and life?

Often our brains stop us from trying something new. They say: I don't have the time, the space, or the knowledge and we feel so overwhelmed that we never start, or worse, we are so full of energy and enthusiasm that our expectations become unsustainable and we feel like failures. Here are some easy ways to make growing your own part of your life today and forever more.

---

[18] Ulrich Schmutz, Margi Lennartsson, Sarah Williams, Maria Devereaux and Gareth Davies 2014. *The benefits of gardening and food growing for health and wellbeing Health Growing Food growing for health and wellbeing* By Garden Organic and Sustain

[19] van den Berg A.E. and M. H. G. Clusters (2011) *Gardening promotes neuroendocrine and affective restoration from stress.* Journal of Health Psychology, 16 (1) 3-11.

1. Plant something

If you have never planted before, start small. What's your favourite herb or what do you spend the most on? For us, it was spending money on fresh herbs and microgreens, like rocket leaves and salads. I found this doubly hard as I hate the fact my greens come in a plastic bag and I never seem to get enough in my veg box. We started small and are now able to plant microgreens every 2 - 3 weeks, which means we have a constant supply, this has been a game changer. Watching our toddler happily pick her food is amazing. It blows my mind that she knows the different types of herbs already. At the grand age of 18 on my gap year I was given some scissors to go and get some rosemary, after 30 mins they asked what on earth I was doing. I was mortified that I had no idea what a rosemary plant looked like, it was pre smartphone days and I was too embarrassed to ask. Now I couldn't imagine not knowing what it is and our two-year old couldn't either.

2. Learn as you go

We learn every single day. Another part of understanding our environment and eating the seasons has been to learn and be curious, a commitment we made when we started foraging. This involves looking up, looking down and looking all around at what nature provides, often in the most unexpected of places.

We decided to learn about one new thing to forage every week. Of course, we wanted to learn every single plant immediately when we first started. That isn't possible, especially when things pop out at different times of year. We learnt more normal ones like Wild Garlic, Elderflowers and Blackberries to begin with and we are slowly building our knowledge year on year to include more plants like Cleavers aka Sticky Willy - did you know you can twist them to extract the juice and you get an espresso like hit when you drink it?

And also Gorse Flowers, which are out in flower most of the year and some people say taste like pineapple or almond or honey. I am not convinced, but they are delicious. As part of our creativity in the kitchen, we have made Gorse Flower Syrup which is great as a cocktail base or added to ice cream. They also look very pretty in ice cubes. The list goes on! Learning as we go means that we learn one thing to forage every week which works out as 52 new opportunities in a year and 104 in two years. It really does build your knowledge in a sustainable way. So, start learning today!

3. Take it easy

We all go into learning with the best intentions (well I am not sure I always had the best intentions at school) but according to the Washington Post less than 10% of people finish online courses[20]. Why is this? We know from decades of research in behaviour change that if we want behaviours to become habits then they need to fit into our lives with minimal mental or physical effort. That means they require less motivation which is good as motivation normally goes up and down. Though often I think I am the only one in the world that happens too!

So a great way to form a new habit is to piggyback the new habit onto something you are already doing. Don't try to learn everything about gardening or seasonal eating in the next ten days! You are setting yourself up to fail. It's all about starting small.

My morning tea was the first habit we decided to piggyback upon. We decided to grow four herbs - Basil, Thyme, Coriander and Rosemary and I would look at them when I had my tea in the

---

[20] Washington Post, Elite Education for the Masses, 2012. https://www.washingtonpost.com/local/education/elite-education-for-the-masses/2012/11/03/c2ac8144-121b-11e2-ba83-a7a396e6b2a7_story.html

morning and make sure I watered them before bed. It has become part of our nightly routine with our toddler, Xanthe. Each week we have planted a little more - it has felt manageable, if not effortless it certainly does not feel like a huge slog - and as we have practiced the habit, it has become part of our daily routine. Now Xanthe's nighttime ritual is to go into the garden, water the plants, talk to them, then upstairs for teeth brushing and a bedtime story. She absolutely loves it. She's even a little confused as to why we don't tuck them into bed every night! Recently we were worried about frost and had no fleece (which is what the pros use, or so I've been told) so we tucked up our tomato plants in a bedsheet weighted down with sand in buckets to protect them from the frost. It felt such an odd thing to be doing but I wanted to protect them as best I could, you see, I'm hooked.

4. Feel connected

Get out there and get the dirt between your hands, use a spade, a trowel, or your largest serving spoon - whatever you like but make sure you feel the earth. There is something so good about being connected with the earth.

Digging around in the dirt is fantastic for some gentle exercise, though once again, start small and don't push yourself. Do what you are comfortable with. Anyone who saw me digging after my c - section would think 'well, she isn't going to get very far' but it wasn't about comparing my progress with anyone else's - it was about my journey. Just digging through that mud made me feel so good! There is another potential benefit to getting your hands dirty - researchers at the University of Bristol[21] reported

---

[21] BBC NEWS | Health | Dirt exposure 'boosts happiness' "Dirt exposure 'boosts happiness" 2007,

that bacteria commonly found living in soil could have a positive effect on our mood, can you believe it! Mice exposed to *Mycobacteruim vaccae* performed better in tests designed to assess the performance of antidepressant drugs. They were shown to have higher levels of serotonin - the brain's "happy" chemical. Of course, we aren't mice and more tests need to be done but it does seem that digging in the dirt can be good for us in more ways than one.

5. Be part of something bigger

The garden isn't static; it is constantly moving. From the changing plants to the colours to the birds that come to visit, I find the ability to be in the moment huge. There are no other distractions - well apart from a toddler trying to sing to the plants to make them grow, or sending buzzing vibes to a bee with a damaged wing so it can get home to its Mummy and Daddy, and then trying to dig some plants up as they aren't growing at the speed she expects so she has decided they will be better somewhere else - maybe she is right.

Finding our local community garden has been life changing for us. We are members of the Abby Physic Garden in Faversham and we learn so much from them every day. There are over a 1000 community gardens and farms across the UK. They are in cities too - even city farms! Spitalfields City Farm in London established the Coriander Club and is renowned for growing Bangladeshi vegetables. The club gives Bangladeshi women, many of them older housewives, the chance to not only grow vegetables, but to get out of the house and meet other people too. For some people it's exactly the community calling they need to make significant life changes. Two brothers we know called David and Terry never really left the house. They then joined the Abby Physic Garden and now say that "we feel we have a purpose in life now we are part of a community and less isolated."

From improving our physical and mental health, to feeding our family, and now concentrating on building our community, we plant it, cook it, and eat it. And we do it together. For me, the biggest thing is the sense of achievement.

Last year, I bought tomato plants for between £2 - £3 each. I left them in their pots and watered them there. I didn't really know how to look after them but still they grew. The excitement I felt picking that first tomato was huge. I savoured every single bite. I didn't grow them from seed but that is something I will work towards. Choose what is right for you. Don't feel overwhelmed by starting. If you have never gardened before, start with your favourite herb - they grow quickly and you can start using them in your kitchen within a month.

Once you start paying attention to your food and growing a little yourself, you are making the biggest commitment to growing your own happiness. It is impossible not to fall in love with those green shoots popping up and the satisfaction of saying 'I grew that'. If you would like more inspiration go to our website www.bangersandballs.co/unlocked and you can download a free guide to getting started. Also feel free to pop Duncan or I a question, we'd love to hear from you.

So, there is something for everyone. Just start.

About the Author

Imogen Tinkler is the Co Founder of Bangers and Balls and the Foodie Revolution along with her husband Duncan Tinkler. Imogen had a successful career in innovation and behaviour change in the not for profit sector - winning multiple awards for her work. Her favourite award was for her work with the Cabinet Office and Co-operative Legal Services on how to implement behaviour change and raise an extra £1 billion a year for charities through legacies in the UK alone.

Imogen draws on many personal experiences from her varied childhood growing up in Essex, Ireland, Pakistan and Australia to connect with people and help to implement changes in their lives in small and manageable ways.

To find out more you can subscribe to her website

www.bangersandballs.co

Or follow them on Facebook www.facebook.com/bangersandballs

Or feel free to drop her a message directly at imogentinkler@gmail.com

Sleeping soundly
by Tracey Allport

How do you feel about sleep?

Is it something you enjoy?

Do you feel that it is a waste of your time that you could be putting to better use?

Do you wake rested or feel that you always need that little bit of extra sleep?

How many hours do you manage each night?

Are you an early bird or a night owl?

These questions demonstrate that we all have a different relationship and view of sleep and what it means to us. Sleep can be affected by so many factors, such as our mood, illness, injury and even our diet.

The definition of sleep

I love to start with a definition; it means we all start from the same place of understanding and sometimes we discover something new.

Wikipedia (2020) states:

> "Sleep is a naturally recurring state of mind and body, characterised by altered consciousnesses, relatively inhibited sensory activity, reduced muscle activity and inhibition of nearly all voluntary muscles during rapid eye movement sleep, and reduced interactions with surroundings. It is distinguished from wakefulness by a decreased ability to react to stimuli, but more reactive than a coma or disorders of consciousness, with sleep displaying very different and active brain patterns."

Why is sleep important?

Sleep is vital to your health, well-being and restoration, physically, cognitively and psychologically.

Did you know that the longest anyone has survived without sleep is just 11 days; after that you will die!

Sleep is important for immunity, reducing your risk of Alzheimer's, increasing your life span, maintaining your weight, your gut microbiome and regulating appetite, healing and repairing bodily tissues and it helps fight inflammation, regulating cholesterol levels and heart health, maintaining concentration and attention, reducing stress, fighting depression, forming new pathways in the brain, it helps with memory consolidation, creativity, learning, processing of information and decision making (Walker 2017). It also improves our quality of life and I think we can all attest to feeling happier and experiencing more vitality after a good shut eye.

Brain cells actually shrink by 60% during sleep, allowing the brain's waste removal system, the glymphatic system, to remove metabolic waste. Our brain's literally remove the garbage at night!

With all of the wonderful reasons sleep benefits us, it makes you wonder why we feel we can take from our sleep stores, without experiencing detrimental effects?

Societal pressures invade our routines and we feel pressured to perform extra tasks, staying longer at work or working from home after our allotted hours. Maybe catching up on chores or trying to create precious quiet time, after the jobs of the day have been completed and the children have gone to bed? We only have so many hours in a day and so we maybe start to steal time, from a part of our day, that we believe could be put to better use.

We can only maintain this thief like approach for a short time, before we start to feel the detrimental effects.

From here on in, your beliefs around sleep need to be positive ones.

Sleep is your friend; it is your natural medicine and it should be your number one priority in life.

I've got rhythm!

Would you describe yourself as a lark or a night owl?

We all have a rhythm that is unique to us and this is because of our natural body clock, sleep-wake cycle, which is an interactive process of circadian rhythms and sleep pressure.

Circadian rhythms are responsible for our level of wakefulness to rise and fall throughout the day. Most people will feel the strongest desire to sleep between 1.00pm and 3.00pm (the post lunch time crash!) and then again between 2.00am and 4.00am, but this can vary from person to person.

The production of Melatonin (the hormone responsible for regulating the sleep-wake cycle) will stop around 7.00am and commence around 9.00pm in preparation for sleep.

Circadian rhythms also change as we age; teenagers struggle with waking and prefer to stay up later, they also need to sleep for longer. As we age our quality of sleep actually improves and so we tend to sleep for less time.

All of our body's functions, such as our immune system, gut function, hormonal system or muscle strength, are controlled in some way by the Suprachiasmatic nucleus (SCN). It is the brain's master body clock and it is influenced by light and dark cycles (not the 24-hour clock). This is why we feel so dysregulated when the clocks change, or we abuse our exposure to light.

Sleep pressure refers to the over-riding build-up of brain pressure, through the release of the chemical Adenosine, creating the need for sleep, brought on by the increasing amount of time spent awake. The release of Adenosine starts from the moment you wake, to the moment you go to sleep and usually takes 12-18 hours, in the majority of people. Drinking caffeine can mute the sleep signal and transversely, avoiding naps and caffeine can increase your sleep pressure.

The stages of sleep

The quality of your sleep is determined by the oscillation between the NREM (slow-wave light and deep sleep) and REM (Rapid eye movement) phases of sleep, which occurs every 90 minutes. There is no scientific consensus as to why we traverse between NREM and REM sleep throughout the night, rather than in a linear fashion. But what we do know is that all types of sleep are important and missing out will lead to deprivation and brain impairment.

Studies have shown that sleep debt is cumulative and cannot be fully repaid by a sneaky lie in at the weekend!

The consequences of sleep deprivation includes an increase in the stress hormone cortisol which raises blood pressure and impairs the body's ability to regulate blood sugar, increased risk of type 2 diabetes, weight gain and increased gut permeability, decreased cognitive ability, poor performance at work, difficulties with decision making and an increased risk of road traffic accidents, there is also an increased chance of psychiatric disorders.

Strategies for a restful sleep

Sleep hygiene is the term that relates to strategies to improve our sleep habits and behaviours.

Amazingly 35 to 50 percent of adults worldwide regularly experience insomnia symptoms.

Establish a routine; rise at the same time each morning and go to bed at a set time in the evening (even at the weekends), as this helps to regulate your body clock and could help you to fall asleep and stay asleep for the night

Exposing ourselves to sunlight first thing in the morning, for 20 minutes, aids our feelings of well-being, increases vitamin D production which contributes to our quality of sleep and resets our circadian rhythm. Try having your morning cuppa in the garden or take the dog (or cat) for a walk, as the sunlight will trigger your brain to wake and start its day. If you don't have time, turn on your brightest light or invest in a daylight bulb.

A short power nap of approximately 20 minutes, during the day, may give you a much-needed boost, but try not to nap after 4pm, or you may struggle to fall asleep at night.

Establish a relaxing wind down routine that works for you. We are all different and some people prefer different sensory input to aid their wind down ritual. E.g. a warm bath, weighted blankets to provide deep stimulation which will settle the sensory/nervous systems, soothing music, meditation or relaxing smells. A relaxing ritual will help you to separate your sleep time from exciting activities and reduce any feelings of anxiety or stress.

Go to sleep when you feel drowsy at night; sounds simple, but we will often fight that feeling for an extra hour to watch something on TV. Listen to your body; it knows what it needs and you're more likely to maintain your circadian rhythm.

Aim for an average of 7-8 hours per night, as an adult.

Ensure you are comfortable and supported in bed. This may sound obvious, but if your mattress is lumpy, or your pillow unsupportive, your body will find it difficult to rest. Poor postures lead to pain and discomfort resulting in a struggle to fall asleep, or wake you prematurely. Sprung mattresses with natural fillings will allow a supported posture and also allow the body to breathe, maintaining its temperature, where foam mattresses will trap body heat, increase perspiration and also cause difficulties with turning, as they tend to create fixed postures, when you sink into the foam. Waking with stiff dead limbs is most unpleasant!

Reduce external stimulation; muffling sounds with soft furnishings in your bedroom, may be helpful, or using ear plugs is the cheapest and easiest way to block out sounds.

White noise machines can help by providing a different sound to focus on, as they emit a constant background noise distracting you from the neighbour's dog or your husband's snoring!

Consider the use of soft focus or dimmable lighting in the bedroom; as they will be easier on the eye and turn off the lights shortly after retiring to bed. Ensure that your room is dark with black out blinds and extra thick curtains, especially invaluable during summer months. Ensure all devices are turned off, as darkness is the signal to our bodies, that it is time to rest and triggers the production of melatonin (the hormone responsible for sleep).

Avoid reading on your mobile phone, tablet or e-reader late at night or in bed, as the device will have a stimulating effect. A good book will help you to drift off easier (as long as it isn't too exciting!)

Avoid using digital screens 2 hours before bed. The blue light that they emit is super stimulating and is on the same wavelength as the morning sun, so you're confusing your brain into believing it is time to wake up! It's also likely that the content from social media, emails etc will have you ruminating on your thoughts and you won't be able to switch off.

Try and avoid watching television 60-90 minutes before bedtime. They emit blue light, but their effects aren't quite as severe as other technology, as they tend to be positioned further away. The amount of light emitted is likely to still have an effect on circadian rhythms and the content you're watching is likely to have your brain whirring! Certainly, avoid watching the news or anything with an emotive content.

If you need to use a light at night, to tend to the children or access the bathroom, use a red night light has it has the least impact on the circadian body clock.

A wake-up alarm light, which simulates sunrise, may be a more pleasing and a less stressful way to wake, especially in the dark winter months.

Clean air helps the environment to be free of toxins and keeps it fresh for sleeping; air purifying plants help to improve air quality and improve unwanted pollutants. Peace lilies and Aloe Vera are particularly good and look beautiful too. Removing tech from the bedroom also helps to improve air quality and using air-purifiers can help to remove air contaminants. Airing your room and having some fresh air at night can also aid a blissful slumber.

Maintain the right temperature; your room ideally should be 60-67 degrees. Use the correct tog duvet for the seasons. We lose

80% of our body heat through a quilt, so have extra blankets available if you are prone to waking due to feeling cold. Using a hot water bottle or bed socks can help if you are prone to feeling cold. If feeling too hot is a problem for you, or you experience night flashes, then using long-staple cotton sheets (cool and breathable), with blankets will allow your body to breathe and to regulate your temperature according to your needs. Lyocell sheets may also be a good consideration, as they are cool, breathable and wick moisture away from the body. New products are also now available, such as temperature regulating duvets and cooling pillows.

Keep your bedroom for bedroom activities! Anchoring your space for relaxation, sex and sleep is vital. If you work on your laptop, in your bed, how can you expect yourself to switch off? Your subconscious mind will automatically believe it is time to fire up and go to work!

Exercise daily; vigorous exercise is best, but any kind of activity is better than no activity, to help you power down! But do avoid exercising 2-3 hours before bed as your nervous system will be too stimulated to calm down.

Avoid caffeine after 2pm and don't drink more than 6 caffeinated drinks in one day. Caffeine is a central nervous system stimulant (Methylxanthine) and it is the world's most widely consumed psychoactive drug. It reversibly blocks the action of adenosine on its receptors and consequently prevents the onset of drowsiness induced by adenosine. Caffeine also stimulates certain portions of the autonomic nervous system. Caffeine has a half-life of 6 hours, based on a 6-ounce cup and 1 milligram of caffeine per millilitre of coffee.

If you're interested in a rough estimate, of the amount of caffeine in your blood stream, then head over to www.perfectcoffathome.com/caffeine-calculator

Scientists have identified a large number of foods containing melatonin (a brain chemical responsible for regulating sleep) that positively impact upon sleep (Meng 2017). Consuming these foods can help to reduce insomnia and improve symptoms of sleep disorders. Good sources of melatonin rich foods include, eggs, fish, nuts, seeds, tart cherries, kiwis and legumes. Tart cherries are in fact the most concentrated source of melatonin in all forms; fresh, dried, frozen or as a juice (Pigeon 2013). Tart cherry juice has also been shown to be comparable with Valerian, which is a well-known herb used to induce sleepiness. It can be taken as a capsule or as a tea; but prepare yourself, as it smells rather like rotten feet!

Researchers have found that Tryptophan stimulates the production of serotonin (a relaxing neurotransmitter) in the brain (Richard 2009). Foods containing tryptophan (an essential amino acid) can be found in milk, oats, red meat, eggs, peanuts, turkey, tuna, bananas and dark chocolate (Strasser 2016).

One study found that consuming bananas for breakfast can help you sleep better at night (they also contain magnesium which has a positive effect on melatonin levels). You need to obtain Tryptophan from your diet and you only require a small amount (250-425mg, which translates to 3.5 to 6.0mg/kg of body weight) per day (Wada 2013).

Eating 2 kiwis 1 hour before bed has been proven to increase sleepiness and to sleep longer with fewer interruptions to your sleep.

Foods that help to increase the relaxing brain neurotransmitter serotonin, are also good to help fall asleep more quickly. Serotonin helps to regulate the sleep/wake cycle and these foods include, oats, fruits, wholegrain foods and nuts (Dugovic 2001). And be aware that caffeine can actually suppress Serotonin levels.

Don't eat a heavy meal within 3 hours of going to bed. When the body is preparing to sleep and we are feeling tired, the body stops producing insulin. We need to try and eat within our natural rhythms.

Stop smoking or vaping as they are linked to a long list of health issues, sleep problems being one of them.

Alcohol is a sedative, you may feel that it helps you fall asleep faster, but it will in fact disrupt the quality of your sleep, as it delays the REM cycle and you won't wake feeling rested; so best avoid the slippery slope of a night cap!

Set aside some time to offload your thoughts or worries, or plan for the next day; a 'brain dump' means you've cleared your mind ready for a restful night.

Ignoring intrusive thoughts may be difficult, so try to focus on something positive. I like to end my day being grateful even for the small things! That way I am focusing on the positives, rather than the negatives. But don't start reliving the day and creating stories in your head!

If you're in the habit of waking at night (remembering something important) jot it down on a notepad, kept next to your bed. That way you know you won't forget it, so it won't keep you awake ruminating.

Don't try hard to fall asleep; the more you battle, the more worked up you will feel. Tell yourself that it's okay to rest your body, even if you are awake.

Never go to bed on an argument; sound advice given to me by my father on my wedding day!

Cognitive behavioural therapy for insomnia (CBT-I) is an approved method for treating insomnia without the use of medication. It is aimed at changing sleep habits and scheduling factors, as well as misconceptions about sleep and insomnia, that perpetuate sleep difficulties. Used in conjunction with meditation and mindfulness it has been shown to improve sleep better than CBT-I alone

Schedule a regular massage; they should be included as part of a regular self-care routine; not only will massage help to reduce anxiety, stress, low mood, and pain, it also aids sleep by increasing serotonin levels (precursor to melatonin).

Aromatherapy; the art and science of using powerful plant-based oils. Essential oils have become increasingly popular over recent years, for those on a quest for healthier options to health and well-being. The aromas can be relaxing, energising and uplifting and work directly through the olfactory nerves to create a brain reaction. It is imperative that you seek advice from a qualified aromatherapist, who will be able to carry out a full consultation and check for contraindications. It is imperative that essential oils are used safely, not ingested or applied neat to the skin; always dilute the oils in a carrier fat, to the correct ratio, before using in the bath or on the body. One of the most renowned essential oils for its sedative effects is Lavender (Lavandula augustifolia). Lavender however can be more stimulating for children with ADHD or Autism and should be avoided in the first trimester of pregnancy. Lavender is actually an adaptogen, which means that it will adapt to the body's physiological processes. So, lavender used in your morning bath will adapt to your body's circadian rhythm and aid a restful night's sleep.

Hypnosis is an extremely powerful tool to change patterns of thought and behaviours, that you want to change. Sleep difficulties are often related to stress, overwhelm or other emotional issues. Your subconscious is the creative part of your mind, that may keep you busy, doing the jobs that it feels it should be doing or trying to solve, even in the middle of the night! One of the most important things that your subconscious needs to be aware of, is that sleep is the most important job and as a CONTROL practitioner I love to empower clients to identify and change the patterns that are contributing to their sleep issues.

Meditation in itself does not induce sleep; it increases our focus but changes our brain waves to create feelings of relaxation, as a bi product. It will help to quieten the mind and enhance calm, by shifting the focus away from a busy worrying mind and physiologically slows breathing, reduces stress hormones, decreases blood pressure, slows the heart rate and increases melatonin and serotonin. Finding a quiet space or lying in bed to perform a body scan meditation, can be the most effective to use at night. As you focus on your breathing and consciously relax each area of your body; if your mind becomes distracted, gently bring yourself back to your body. You can of course use a guided meditation or try binaural beats (wearing headphones is required), which will change the brainwave patterns to induce sleep.

Try this simple breathing technique 4-10 times maximum, whilst lying in bed. Breath in through your nose for a count of 4, hold the breath for a count of 7 and exhale slowly for a count of 8. It can take a little practice initially. It is important not to exceed the recommended 10 repetitions, as this exercise has a direct effect on the autonomic nervous system.

If you feel that your sleep is impacting your function, keep a sleep diary for two weeks, which will provide useful objective feedback to your GP or health professional, who can then discuss your sleep habits and evaluate any common patterns or issues that you may be experiencing.

Sleep is a wonderful gift that we all need to embrace, to gain the maximum quality and feel good factor from our lives. Remember that sleep is your friend, so don't sacrifice the relationship for anything!

If you would like to discuss strategies to help with sleep or any of the treatments that I can provide, (Occupational Therapy, Remedial Hypnosis/The CONTROL System, Aromatherapy, Massage therapies and Meditation), then please contact me by email or via my website.

Please email tracey@moththerapies.co.ukif you would like a free body scan audio meditation, or a meditation e-book sent to you.

About the Author

Tracey is a master of mind and body therapies, supporting women who experience stress, overwhelm, anxiety or burnout.

Having qualified as an Occupational Therapist, some 28 years ago and worked primarily in the fields of neurology, acquired brain injury and mental health, she went on to study coaching, remedial hypnosis, and complementary therapies, including massage, aromatherapy and meditation, to be able to provide comprehensive therapeutic interventions and breakthrough coaching conversations.

MOTH Therapies offers tailor made services to clients, who are proactive and want to be self-empowered to make changes, so that they feel in control of themselves again.

Based in her beautiful bespoke studio in Whitstable, for face to face connections, or virtually if you are further afield.

Contact details:

Website: www.moththerapies.co.uk
Facebook: www.facebook.com/moththerapies
Instagram: www.instagram.com/moth_therapies
Linkedin: Tracey (Reay) Allport
Email: tracey@moththerapies.co.uk

References:

Dugovic, C. (2001), 'Role of serotonin in sleep mechanisms', *Revue Neurologique*, 157(11). Available at: http://europepmc.org/article/med/11924032 (Accessed: 15 May 2020).

Meng, X., Li, Y. and Li, H.B. (2017) 'Dietary sources and Bioactivities of Melatonin', *Nutrients*, 9(4), p. 367.

Pigeon, W.R. et al. (2013) 'Effects of tart cherry juice beverage on the sleep of older adults with insomnia: a pilot study', *Journal of Medicinal Food*, 13(3), pp. 579-583.

Strasser, B. et al. (2016) 'Mood, Food, and cognition: role of Tryptophan and serotonin', *Current Opinion in Clinical Nutrition and Metabolic Care*, 19(1), 00. 55-61.

Richard, D.M. et al. (2009) 'L-Tryptophan: Basic Metabolic functions, behavioural research and therapeutic indications', *International Journal of Tryptophan Research*, 2, pp. 45-60.

Wada, K. et al. (2013) 'A tryptophan-rich breakfast and exposure to light with low colour temperature at night improve sleep and salivary melatonin level in Japanese students', *Journal of Circadian Rhythms*, 11(4), doi: 10.1186/1740-3391-11-4.

Wikipedia (2020) *Sleep*. Available at: https://en.wikipedia.org/wiki/Sleep (Accessed: 15 May 2020).

Walker, M. (2017) *Why we sleep*. Allen Lane.

Maintaining a Positive State of Mind

By Sacha Mulligan

Introduction

In my work, my aim is to facilitate the restoration, reframing and rebooting of a client's life in areas where they may be struggling with issues such as self-esteem, lack of confidence and emotional wellbeing. During my consultations I teach tried and trusted techniques to help boost the physical and financial aspects of clients' lives, and assist them in regaining full control once again by the use of Positive Psychology.

Positive Psychology began as a domain of psychology in 1998, when the celebrated and respected American psychologist Martin Seligman chose it as his theme of practice during his term as president of the American Psychological Association.

Positive Psychology is the study of all the positive aspects of the human experience that make life worth living. The greater emphasis is put on the good things that are present in our lives and encourages changes for the better. Changing the mindset of individuals, communities and even organisations can enable them to thrive and work in a more productive and harmonious way. The basic area of study focuses on positive emotions such as contentment with the past, current happiness levels, and hopes and aspirations for the future. The study goes further to include positive character traits such as courage, resilience, curiosity, self-knowledge, integrity, compassion and creativity. When Positive Psychology is employed thoughtfully, it can result in an individual becoming much happier and more contented with their day-to-day living. If the main focus is placed on turning a negative into a positive, positivity eventually prevails over time.

As we are all trying to cope in these unsettled times due to the pandemic, I want to share my tools and techniques with you to demonstrate how to stay in a positive state of mind as you return to the workplace, learn about yourself, work on yourself daily, make yourself a priority, and the ripple effect that happens when staying in this positive mindset.

Gratitude

The first step everyone needs to take is to be grateful right now, this very minute. Be grateful that you can return to work, as there are so many who have not been given the opportunity to do so. Then look around you and see what you have in your life, and ask what you are grateful for. The air you breathe, the bed you have slept in, your home, the trees that provide the oxygen for you to breathe, your family and friends, your health and that of your family, and the food that you eat. These are just a few things that might be on your list.

When we are in a state of gratitude we cannot be in a negative mindset. It is a fact that the frontal lobe of our brain controls important cognitive skills in humans such as emotional expression, memory, problem solving, language, judgement and sexual behaviour. Being grateful shifts your emotional state towards positivity. Gratitude coupled with the challenges and obstacles that we face and overcome helps to bring balance into our lives.

Hopefully, we learn lessons from dealing with these situations and these experiences help us to develop and grow. A life without challenges begins and ends in the graveyard! Therefore it is very important that the first thing you do each morning and the last thing you do each night is to write a list of things that you are grateful for – the effect of physically writing a list is more profound than simply reading it, or indeed just saying it. It can also help us to have a better night's sleep when we can look at the positive things in our lives from the day that has just passed. It is also vital to learn about yourself. When we focus on self-awareness we grow as people, and this is also the case when we become aware of our thoughts and feelings. Reflect daily on the things that work for you and those that don't. I do this exercise to stop myself from making the same mistakes and expecting a different outcome!

Ask yourself these questions each day:

- What has worked for me?
- What hasn't worked for me?
- How do I feel?
- What can I celebrate?
- What do I need to keep doing to stay positive?
- If you have suffered from stress during that day, ask yourself why. Be aware of the trigger that put the wheels in motion and see if the reason can be changed.

I question everything in my daily life and make choices based on what is right for me. If I later find that I have made the wrong decision, I don't beat myself up about it; I just ask myself, "What can I learn from this?"

When we ask ourselves questions our brain has a tendency to supply us with the answers that we seek.

Visualisation

Another powerful tool is to use visualisation – if you visualise exactly how you wish your day to go, sit quietly and mentally send the intention out that you want to have a good day, or even a great night's sleep, your request will be realised, providing you can clearly see the events unfolding in your mind's eye. Visualising is also a great way to learn about yourself. Don't hold back from dreaming of what you want to achieve in life.

Working on Yourself

An additional important daily activity is to work on yourself. I do an exercise each day that involves my four GEMS, as I call them:

> G – gratitude, which we have already covered.
>
> E – exercise. It is imperative to do some form of exercise each day to release the serotonin that we need to keep happy and to remain feeling good. Not only will it help to keep you healthy, but it will also boost your immune system and during this crisis that is a valuable resource. The additional benefit of exercising is the sense of achievement you get when you have completed a session.
>
> M – meditation. I meditate twice a day – twenty minutes in the morning and twenty minutes in the afternoon. I practice transcendental meditation, which assists in clearing the subconscious mind so any old and redundant thought patterns that emerge and keep us rooted

in outmoded mindsets can be cleared away with practice. It is a great feeling to be able to clear your mind. If you visit my website www.sachamariemulligan.com there is a free download that you can listen to with instructions on what to do. If you were to tell me that you were unable to meditate twice a day for twenty minutes, I would suggest that perhaps you need to meditate for at least an hour per day! You can listen and meditate while travelling on public transport during your commute to and from work if need be.

S – self-love. In my view this is the most important area to work on and assists in building self-confidence. The exercise here is to use the power of affirmations. These are things that you want to be, now or in the future. At first, affirmations can be difficult to believe in, but I have the answer to help with this. Start by repeating the two words that are both powerful and instrumental in the process of changing your mindset - I AM.

- I am enough
- I am happy
- I am calm
- I am beautiful
- I am successful
- I am a positive person
- I am a hard worker who enjoys everything that I do

These are just some examples, but I cannot stress strongly enough how this exercise has transformed my life, and the lives of many others who I have had the privilege of working with. If you find it hard to believe at first, which initially is probable, ask yourself why. Your brain will supply you with the answer. So for example:

- Why am I enough?
- Why am I happy?
- Why am I calm?
- Why am I beautiful?
- Why am I a hard worker who enjoys everything I do?

The brain is a very powerful piece of equipment, and in point of fact we tend to believe everything we tell ourselves. The good thing is that we can also trick our brain into believing that something is already true even if it is not the case yet.

Try these GEMS for the next thirty days and see how you feel afterwards. However, I recommend that you continue to do the exercises for longer, and include this practice as a way of life. For the past ten years I have done so each day.

Summary

Make yourself a priority and know that you are the most important person in your life. If you work on yourself first, the benefits will also be felt by those around you. If you make time to do these exercises each day it will help you face challenges and difficulty with confidence. You are important, so start believing it and make yourself your first priority. Of course your family are important and I am not suggesting otherwise, and so is your job and career, but you do need, as they say, to fill your cup first to ensure that you have the inner resources to deal with anything that arises, and that can be achieved by having a positive mindset. Our lives have been turned upside down during this crisis, and many changes have had to be made, so achieving the best mindset is key. I have had clients who have been laid off, or have lost their jobs completely, and these daily exercises have prevented them from reverting to the damaging habits of their past, such as alcohol abuse, drugs and gambling. This is all because they have worked on themselves and therefore avoided regressing to previous life choices.

When you embrace this daily routine, I can assure you that the improvements will not only benefit you, but also those around you - or as I term it, the 'Ripple Effect.' You will find that the improvements that you experience will flow throughout your life. Those you choose to spend time with will be more positively aware, as you will be, and in turn like concentric circles in a body of water, the ripple effect will then have a bearing on those around them, and so on.

As I explained previously, this is a way of life, and it is about taking action to improve the areas of your life that you have found wanting. Do the work daily and see what happens around you. I can promise you that it will be worth it.

Give it a try.

About the Author

I am Sacha Marie Mulligan and I am a Positive Psychology Practitioner. I am also a Counsellor, Life Coach and Human Behaviour Practitioner with over twenty years' experience in the field. I work with clients either on a one-to-one basis or as part of a group, and how I work depends entirely on the individual needs of the client I am helping.

In my sessions I focus on four areas of wellness – financial, physical, mental and emotional. In my own life I have had to face and overcome major obstacles, and I therefore believe that I have had first-hand experience of some of the issues that many people in our society have to face daily. In the past I have had to battle my own very serious demons, and I have recovered from drug addiction, alcohol abuse, anxiety, depression, lack of confidence, low self-esteem, post-natal depression, PTSD (Post Traumatic Stress Disorder) and the personal grief I suffered following the death of a much loved boyfriend. I realise that this is a rather daunting and comprehensive list, but as I say, I do like to try everything once! I am living proof that the techniques that I teach actually work, and I am now flourishing and am happier now than I have ever been. It has been my pleasure to help hundreds of people over the years to develop calm, happy, peaceful and more balanced lives than they previously had. I find the transformation very inspiring. I often have the honour to be invited by CEOs of companies to speak to their workforce with a view to improving the positive mindset of the employees and ultimately increasing the productivity of the company. It is always a privilege to have the opportunity to draw on my twenty-eight years of experience within the personal development world, so that I can help people to work on areas of their lives with which they are dissatisfied, and bring about a positive change for the better.

If you wish to contact me directly to learn more about my work, please either follow me on Facebook or Instagram (Sacha Marie Mulligan), or contact me via my website www.sachamariemulligan.com. You can also email me at sachamariemulligan@icloud.com

Lessons from Evidence Based Supported Employment - A Surviving and Thriving at Work Toolkit
by Paul Dorrington

In this book, you will have heard from many experts in their field, and you will come across strategies and tools to use, from stress management, nutrition, sleep science, complementary therapies and many other pearls of wisdom.

Well, this is your toolkit which you can use and store the tools of your trade.

Resilience is not some superhuman ultra-tough exterior in which the challenges of life bounce off us. We are humans, not robots, and cycles of low energy are essential for regenerating new energy and weathering these ebbs and flows are essential for maintaining consistent holistic health and well-being.

Real resilience warrants courage.

The courage to be vulnerable; the courage to be imperfect, the courage to be a human being with the limits that come with this, and in this space, we can find our power.

In human terms, healthy levels of stress are essential for physical and mental well-being, whereas overworking and excessive stress is proven to have a detrimental effect on physical and mental health, which you will learn more about from other specialist chapters.

My specialist area is helping people take back control of their working lives and consequentially own their life in straight forward practical ways that enable them to manage work and life stress in real time.

This chapter is no replacement for evidence-based therapy, psychiatric or psychological therapy, and I would recommend that you access professional support and help if you are experiencing mental or physical ill health, as these interventions can be integrated into your recovery and toolkit, as well as any spiritual or deeply personal ways you have decided to manage and overcome challenges you may have with mental ill health. One of the key principles that evidence-based supported employment teaches is integrating professional clinical support in any work, and wellbeing plan is a key component in true success, whether it is a GP or other relevant specialist.

My aim in this chapter is to take you away from complex theory, to the day to day application of mentally healthy living.

If you have more challenging and complex mental health issues, these treatments or therapies can be integrated into this toolkit, and whether it is time off for a medical appointment and blood test, psychological therapy or a spiritual or holistic therapy, time and time again, these toolkits prove when you fit individual person's needs and challenges into this model, rather than trying to fit a model onto a person by giving advice, the uniqueness flows into a successful work life balance, and that is where the genius lies, in its very simplicity.

When I was asked to write this chapter, I thought of what I could share that would have the most value and be applicable and universal for people wanting to learn to have a happy healthy working life. This has traditionally been a very difficult question to answer as people are so different, their gender, personality style, sexuality, spiritual beliefs, religious beliefs, cultural deference, etc. My head and heart already knew the answer.

In early 2000, I joined the UK National Health Service initiative to develop evidence-based, supported employment services in London. It was there that I met Dr Rachel Perkins OBE, and during this time I was deeply inspired by her openness in regards to disclosing her own mental health issues, her ground-breaking insights and activism for equality and human rights for people who experience mental ill health.

After directly experiencing the power of supported employment to overcome my own mental health condition, I was hooked. This in turn inspired me to devote my life to a profession that quite literally uses work to help people build and rebuild their working lives with meaning and purpose.

I spent the subsequent years working with organisations and businesses all over London, helping their employees to survive and thrive at work and to overcome or manage the adversity of experiencing severe and enduring mental ill health.

No longer were people too sick to work - they could manage their health and their work together.

The teams that I led went on to successfully support many hundreds of people back into the workplace, either by getting new jobs or starting businesses, or holding onto the jobs or businesses they already had.

By using Surviving and Thriving methodology and toolkits, we were able to help people take back control of their working lives, develop a healthy work-life balance and recognise unique self-management strategies, whilst at the same time work with their managers, occupational health and human resources.

This in turn would encourage the integration of well-being strategies into their daily working lives and demands, while navigating the challenges associated with clinical and psychological support.

I have supported a wide variety of occupations from CEO's and construction workers, police officers, to doctors, nurses, accountants, administrators and all levels in between; time and time again people across all industries have demonstrated that with the right strategies and support, people can successfully gain, retain and sustain meaningful employment.

When I began using Dr. Rachel Perkins' Surviving and Thriving toolkits, I quickly realised how universal these toolkits were. Not only were they applicable to people rebuilding their lives after mental ill health, they were applicable to anyone wanting to build a mentally healthy working life.

They provide a framework for integrated work-life balance strategies, while supporting managers and leaders to collaborate in creative ways to support their employees with a healthy working life and well-being, which naturally has a positive and creative impact on their performance.

I want to thank the former Royal Association for Disability Rights for their permission to adapt and use these toolkits for the businesses and individuals I work with, in order to develop mentally healthy working practices and well-being strategies.

I also want to give a special thanks to their author for permission to use your toolkits in Phoenix Transformational Services, my long-time mentor and friend, Dr Rachel Perkins OBE. You believed in me when others didn't. My promise to you, to share our gifts and learning to all those who can benefit.

How to use this toolkit

The toolkit contains a number of sections, but every one of us is different so all our plans need to be individual to us. You may wish to use a different format and/or only use some of the sections we have suggested – that is fine!

- Some people may prefer to develop a plan to manage the stresses and strains of work on their own. However, line managers share responsibility for the health and well-being of their staff. If you want help and support from your manager then it is important to discuss with them the ways in which they can best support your well-being and performance at work.
- If you do create a plan with your manager then it should be confidential between the two of you and should not appear in your staff record.
- Prevention is better than cure - it is usually best to prepare plans in advance rather than wait until problems arise. However, these plans should be living documents that you review regularly and update in the light of experience. Supervision and appraisal meetings offer a good opportunity to develop and review plans.
- In general the more specific you can be about what you will do and what your manager can do to help the more likely your plan is to be successful.
- If you are a business owner or entrepreneur, how could you adapt this toolkit to your lifestyle? And if so and you are your own manager, could you use the managers section in this toolkit to manage yourself with the same care and compassion that you expect others to have with you?

Think creatively in the modern age!

- Could you include plans for working from home and remote working?
- Could you include time to touch base with colleagues via Skype, Zoom or phone?
- If you are working remotely, could you include end of day catch ups with your manager or colleagues to offload and reflect on the challenges of the day?
- If you are working remotely, could you schedule down time, rest or take exercise breaks and get some fresh air?
- If you are receiving therapy or treatments in relation to mental or physical ill health, can you include specific advice from your clinicians or schedule time for therapy or medical appointments or picking up prescriptions?
- Are there any specific routines or strategies to include to manage other disabilities; physical/sensory/learning impairments, such as equipment or in work support?

Your Turn

The pages that follow are a blank canvas in which I encourage you to be honest and creative. In life we often join the dots by looking backwards. But masterpieces are not, join the dots. They take honesty, authenticity and passion.

Before you begin your personalised toolkit, I want to take this time to wish you the best on your journey and say no job, work or business is worth your health. I say to you with faith, if you ever estimate how much money you are worth in work or business; I have one answer for you all. You are priceless.

With love
Paul Dorrington

Part 1: A Work Health And Well-Being Promotion Plan

It is not easy to juggle the demands of your job and the demands of other things outside work that are important to you. A health and well-being promotion plan helps you to strike a balance and remain on an even keel at work.

It might be useful to think about:

1. **The things that are important to your life outside work** (like sports, hobbies and spending time with your partner or children) and when you are going to make time for them.

2. **Things you need to do every day or week to keep yourself feeling on top of things.**

   For example:
   - Get up in time to have a proper breakfast
   - Have a lie in at least once a week
   - Take a lunch break out of the workplace
   - Get some exercise every day
   - Allot a set time to answer e-mails and write up notes each day at work
   - Have a 'treat' – something to look to – every day/week

3. **Things your manager can do to help you stay on an even keel at work.**

   For example:
   - Let me have Wednesday evenings off for my yoga class
   - Help me to prioritise when I have too much to do
   - Say 'thank you' when I have done something he/she asked
   - Encourage me to tell him/her when I am having difficulties
   - Recognise my need to pray
   - Make any adjustments I need because of a health condition, impairment or responsibilities outside work

My Work Health And Well-Being Promotion Plan

The things that are important to me in my life outside work (and when I will do them)

The things I need to do every day or week to keep myself on an even keel	The things that my manager can do to help me stay on an even keel at work

Part 2: A Work Health And Well-Being First Aid Kit

It is almost inevitable that we will sometimes feel upset, discouraged, hopeless, angry, worried or stressed out at work. We have first aid boxes for minor physical cuts and bruises - this is a first aid kit for the emotional cuts and bruises.

It might be useful to think about:

1. Things you can do while you are actually at work when you feel upset, discouraged, hopeless, angry, anxious or stressed out

    For example:
    - Have a cup of coffee or tea
    - Talk to a friend on the phone at lunch-time
    - Get out of the situation for a while (maybe by going out for a break or even just going to the toilet for a bit of peace and quiet)
    - Think about something you are looking forward to

2. Things you can do after work so that you don't take the troubles of the day home with you

    For example:
    - Talk through the events of the day with colleagues before you go home
    - Take a walk – get some fresh air
    - Go to the gym - get some exercise
    - Listen to music
    - Read a book or newspaper
    - Play your favourite computer game
    - Have a long hot bath

My Work Health And Well-Being First Aid Kit

Things I can do to get myself back on an even keel if I feel upset, discouraged, hopeless, angry, worried or stressed out at work

Things I can do after work so that I don't take the troubles of the day home with me

Part 3: Plan For Managing Things That Get To You At Work

There will always be things that happen at work that knock us off balance and wear us down at work: things that make us feel angry, hurt, upset, discouraged, anxious, stressed out. If we can identify these, we can work out how to stop them getting to us too much.

1. They might be things relating to your job and things your colleagues and managers do like:

- A customer gets angry when we are busting a gut to help them
- Someone complains about our work
- A colleague promises to do something and fails to do it
- We do something we have been asked to do and no-one says 'thank you'
- Colleagues or managers act in a way that seems unfair

For each thing that knocks you off balance, it might be useful to think about:

1. **Things that you can do for yourself that help stop what has happened getting to you too much.** There may be things in your 'first aid kit' that would help.

For example:

- Tell myself that the person was cross because of what had happened to them and that they did not really mean to upset me
- Talk to my colleagues or my manager about how I am feeling
- Do some breathing exercises
- Arrange a treat for myself after work

2. They might be things that happen outside work which have a detrimental impact on you at work like:
- Having a row with our partner
- Money problems
- A loved pet getting sick or dying

2. Things you can ask your manager to do to help you to get back on an even keel

For example:
- Ask me how things are going when he/she notices I am not looking myself (remember to say how they will know)
- In one to one meetings, ask me about jobs I am finding challenging, empathise with the difficulties I am having and help me to think of ways forward
- Make a point of congratulating me for work I have done well

Plan For Managing Things That Get To Me At Work

Things that make me feel angry, hurt, upset, discouraged, anxious, stressed out at work	What I will do to stop it getting to me too much when these things happen	What my manager can do to help me

Part 4: Plan For What To Do When You Are Not Feeling 100% - Having an Off Day

Everyone has their off days – if we can spot that it is a bad day and nip things in the bud then we can stop everything from escalating and going from bad to worse.

First, it is helpful to think about how you will spot when you are having an off day – those tell-tale signs – thoughts, feelings and behaviours – that you are not feeling 100%.

For example:
- Ruminating on something that has happened – going over and over it
- Finding it unusually hard to get up and get going in the morning
- Feeling agitated and unable to relax
- Getting irritable and oversensitive
- Feeling restless and unable to relax

Then it might be useful to think about:

1. **Things you can do to help you cope and get back on an even keel.**

For example:
- Plan something nice for the evening – this might be something small like a long hot bath, or my favourite TV programme
- Talk to a close friend or colleague
- Do something I love – walking in nature, gardening, seeing a great film...
- Plan my next holiday

2. **Things that your manager can do to help you get back on top of things**

For example:
- Try to notice when I am not my usual self and ask if there is anything they can do to help
- Encourage me to approach him/her when I am having problems ... and respond to my requests for help
- Help me prioritise what really needs to be done today
- Encourage me to leave work on time

My Plan For What To Do When I Am Having an Off Day - Not Feeling 100%

How I will know that I am not 100% - the tell- tale signs that all is not well	Things I will do to help me get back on top of things	What my manager can do to help me

Part 5: Plan For What To Do When Everything Is Getting Too Much For You

No matter how much we try to keep on an even keel, all of us get to the point at some time when we have had enough and just want to jack it all in – when everything is getting too much for us and we cannot see a way through. Asking for help can be hard!

First, it is helpful to think about how you will spot when things are not going right for you – those signs – thoughts, feelings and behaviours – that things really are getting too much

For example:

- Disturbed sleep patterns
- Thinking that there is no point in what we are doing
- Getting all sorts of colds and minor infections
- Not hungry - or over-eating to comfort ourselves
- Drinking too much
- Bursting into tears or flying off the handle at the slightest provocation
- Letting responsibilities slip

Then it might be useful to think about:

1. **Things you can do to start putting things right.** There may be things in your 'first aid kit' that would help.

For example:
- Confide in my family and friends and ask for help
- Cut down on social activities
- Try to get some regular exercise – even just a bit
- Talk to my manager about how I am feeling and ask for relief of some responsibilities
- Ask for some leave so I can get away for a bit
- Go and see my GP

2. **Things that your manager can do to help**

For example:
- Make time for me to talk about the difficulties I am having
- Arrange for me to take a few days off
- Help me to reduce my workload while at home some of the time
- Make sure that I only work my set hours
- Remind me of all the good work I have done/that I am a valued member of the team

How I can tell when things really are getting too much for me	Things I will do to help me cope and get back on top of things	What my manager can do to help

About the author
Paul Dorrington

Mental health recovery and vocational rehabilitation specialist, professional speaker and NHS lead.

Winner of the 2019 International Coaching Academy Award for services to the mental health and work and well-being industry.

Winner of the 2019 NHS Chief Executive's Leadership Award.

Paul started his career in 1993 in young people's mental health, drug and alcohol services where he was trained and practised as a counsellor and a street-based outreach worker and service leader in South West London.

While teaching drugs education and harm reduction workshops in public and private schools, he worked with hard to reach socially excluded young people. He referred them back into counselling to help them break the cycle of drug use with the aim of reintegrating them into mainstream society.

In 2002, he joined the NHS, where he pioneered and implemented the Individual Placement and Support model of evidence-based vocational rehabilitation in adult psychiatric services in London. It is now universally known as the most effective model in the world.

In March 2014, Paul founded his own business Phoenix Transformational Services (PTS). PTS works with individuals to develop a mentally healthy culture and practice. This will help them build or rebuild meaningful working lives and businesses so they can have a high-performing and resilient workforce.

'I work with companies committed to real and lasting change and the betterment and well being of staff at all levels of their organisation.' – Paul Dorrington.

Paul's vision is to help companies integrate surviving and thriving toolkits, mental recovery and vocational rehabilitation plans alongside leadership support to integrate preventive and proactive mental health work and well-being strategies from within. He also strives to equip leaders, line managers and staff with effective line management insight, skills, tools and resources to support staff with mental health issues at all stages and develop recovery-based support systems and toolkits.

'My vision when building my own company was to use what I have learned over the years to help integrate preventative strategies, tools and methods into workplace culture and staff across organisations, and preventatively rather than reactively support people in achieving a mentally healthy working life.' – Paul Dorrington.

To find out more about working with the Phoenix Transformational Services team, contact us by phone, email, or visit our website for more information about our services and how to apply to work with us

Email: info@phoenixtransforms.com **Phone:** 0208 943 2637
Facebook: @phoenixtransforms
LinkedIn: http://linkedin.com/in/phoenixtransforms
www.PhoenixTransformationalServices.com

Testimonial

Dr Jo Turner

MBBS MRCPsych CBT Dip/Consultant Psychiatrist
Paul is an innovator and a leader in the field of mental health Vocational Rehabilitation. I worked with him in a Community Mental Health Team for several years and his enthusiastic, can-do attitude gets incredible results. Return to some form of employment is, in my view, just as important, if not more important, than any medication or therapy I can provide as a psychiatrist.

> You have now reached the end of the book.
> We hope that it has provided you with the insight,
> inspiration and tools to make positive and
> lasting changes in your life.

Printed in Great Britain
by Amazon